REED'S HEAD LIGHT,

FOR

Locomotive Engineers

AND MACHINISTS.

COMPRISING SUCH INFORMATION AS NECESSARY TO GIVE A GENERAL KNOWLEDGE OF THE CALCULATION AND CONSTRUCTION OF THE AMERICAN LOCOMOTIVE ENGINE, AND EXPLANATION OF THE LINK AND SLIDE VALVE, AND THEIR WORKING CENTRES; ILLUSTRATING THEIR MOVEMENTS, WITH WORKING VALVE TABLES OF THE LINK MOTION, SHOWING THE EFFECTS PRODUCED IN THE DISTRIBUTION OF STEAM, WITH DIFFERENT DIMENSIONS OF LAPS, LEADS & TRAVELS OF VALVES. PRACTICAL MODE OF SETTING VALVES AND EQUALIZING THE CUT OFF.

PRACTICAL INSTRUCTIONS TO MANAGE THE LOCOMOTIVE.

BY

WM. W. REED,

Mechanical Engineer.

Attempt the end, and never stand to doubt;
Nothing so hard, but search will find it out.

PATERSON, N. J.:
"PRESS" STEAM BOOK AND JOB PRINTING HOUSE, MAIN ST.,
1874.

TO

The Locomotive Engineer,

AS A

TESTIMONIAL of esteem, and admiration of his nobleness and steadiness of nerve, who controlls the power of the Locomotive when at his post of duty, and in whose care the lives of many depends,

THIS VOLUME,

Describing the Locomotive Steam Engine, one of the greatest works of man, by a Brother Engineer,

THE AUTHOR.

PREFACE.

I HAVE written this Book by the request of many Engineers and Machinists, who have desired me to get up a work on the American Locomotive Engine, in such manner that all interested may understand it. I give here the knowledge, from my experience of twenty-two years, as Practical Locomotive Engineer and Machinist. And I have taken care to present it in such a manner as to place within the reach of every Engineer and Machinist a general knowledge of the Locomotive Link and Slide Valve and their motion, and a comprehensive view of the causes which regulate the distribution of steam, and the form and dimensions of the Locomotive Engine, using the simple rules of arithmetic, which are familiar to all: Addition, Subtraction, Multiplication and Division, with tables of different valve motion, showing the effect of Laps, Leads and Travel of Valve; in such a manner that the apprentice can easily understand. Also the management of the Locomotive from practice.

There are many valuable works on the steam engine, but they are, in general, so complicated that a novice can scarcely comprehend the meaning of the terms used. There are also many other works which profess to accomplish this object, but they have fallen far short of giving the desired information. Many of them are mere compilations from theory, having a great many scientific errors; so that these works claim but little attention from one in search of this knowledge. I have given the different parts relating to the construction of the Locomotive and its workings.

I hope my feeble efforts of many hours of hard labor may not only prove of value to all who may seek after the science, but in the description given. I trust a general idea may be had of the art as well as the science.

REED'S

HEAD LIGHT.

TROY WEIGHT.

Troy weight is the weight used in weighing gold, silver and precious stones, diamonds excepted.

24 grains make	1 pennyweight.	pwt.
20 pennyweights make	1 ounce.	oz.
12 ounces make	1 pound.	lb.

—— :o: ——

APOTHECARIES.

This is the same as Troy weight, but differently divided, and is used in mixing medicines.

20 grains make	1 scruple.	sc.
3 scruples make	1 drachm.	dr.
8 drachms make	1 ounce.	oz.

—— :o: ——

AVOIRDUPOIS.

This weight is used in almost all commercial transactions, and in the common dealings of life.

16 drachms make	1 ounce.	oz.
16 ounces make	1 pound.	lb.
25 pounds make	1 quarter.	qr.
4 quarters make	1 hundred.	cwt.
20 hundred weight make	1 ton	T.

Dr.	Oz.	Lb.	Qr.	Cwt.	T.
16	1				
256	16	1			
6,400	400	25	1		
25,600	1,600	100	4	1	
512,000	32,000	2,000	80	20	1

——:o:——

LONG MEASURE.

12	inches (in.) make	1 foot.	ft.
3	feet make	1 yard.	yd.
5½	yards, or 16½ feet, make	1 rod or pole.	rd.
40	rods make	1 furlong.	fr.
8	furlongs, or 320 rods, make	1 mile.	m.
3	miles make	1 league.	lea.
69	1-6 miles, nearly, make	1 degree.	deg.
360	degrees make	1 circle of the earth.	

In.	Ft.	Yd.	Rd.	Fr.	M.
12	1				
36	3	1			
198	16½	5½	1		
7,920	660	220	40	1	
63,360	5,280	1,760	320	8	1

SQUARE MEASURE,

Or Measure of Surfaces.

144 square inches make	1 square foot.	ft.
9 square feet make	1 square yard.	yd.
30¼ square yards, or 272¼ square feet,	1 sqr. rod or pole.	p
40 square rods or poles make	1 rood.	R.
4 roods or 160 poles make	1 acre.	A.
640 acres make	1 square mile.	

In.	Ft.	Yd.	P.	R.	A.	S.M
144	1					
1,296	9	1				
39.204	272¼	30¼	1			
1,568.160	10,890	1.210	40	1		
6,272,640	43,560	4,840	160	4	1	
4,014,489,600	27,878,400	3,097 600	102,400	2,560	640	1

———:o:———

CUBIC, OR SOLID MEASURE.

Is used in measuring such bodies or things as have length, breadth and thickness.

1,728 cubic inches make	1 cubic foot.	cu. ft.
27 cubic feet make	1 cubic yard.	cu. yd.
40 cubic feet make	1 cubic ton.	T.
16 cubic feet make	1 cord foot.	c. ft.
8 cord feet, or 128 cubic feet,	1 cord of wood.	c.

In.	Ft.	Yd.	T.	C.
1,728	1			
46,656	27	1		
69,120	40	1 13-27	1	
221,184	128	4 20-27	3 1-5	1

WINE MEASURE.

4 gills (gi.) make	1 pint.	pt.
2 pints make	1 quart.	qt.
4 quarts make	1 gallon.	gal.
63 gallons make	1 hogshead.	hhd.
2 hogsheads make	1 pipe or butt.	pi.
2 pipes make	1 tun.	tun.

Gi.	Pt.	Qt.	Gal.	Hhd.	Pi.	Tun.
4	1					
8	2	1				
32	8	4	1			
2,016	504	252	63	1		
4,032	1,008	504	126	2	1	
8,064	2,016	1,008	252	4	2	1

The standard unit of liquid measure, adopted by the Government of the United States, is the Winchester wine gallon, which contains 231 cubic inches. The imperial gallon, now adopted in Great Britain, contains 277 274-1000. The standard gallon measures 231 cubic inches, and contains 8.33 avoirdupois pounds of distilled water, at 39 °82-100 Fahrenheit, the barometer at 30 inches.

The gallon of the State of New York contains 8 lbs. pure water, at a maximum density, 221 184-1000.

——:o:——

BEER MEASURE

2 pints (pts.) make	1 quart.	qt,
4 quarts make	1 gallon.	gal.

54 gallons make 1 hogshead. hhd.

Pt.	Qt.	Gal.	Hhd.
2	1		
8	4	1	
432	216	54	1.

——:o:——

DRY MEASURE.

This measure is used in measuring grain, fruit, salt, coal, etc.

2 pints make	1 quart.	qt.
8 quarts make	1 peck.	pk.
4 pecks make	1 bushel.	bus.
8 bushels make	1 quarter.	qr.
36 bushels make	1 chaldron.	ch.

Pt.	Qt.	Pk.	Bu.	Ch.
2	1			
16	8	1		
64	32	4	1	
2304	1152	144	36	1

The standard bushel of dry measure adopted by the United States government in form of a cylinder, is 18 1-2 inches in diameter, and 8 inches deep, containing 2,150 42-100 cubic inches. The Imperial Bushel of Great Britian contains 2,218 196-1000 cubic inches. The standard gallon of United States contains 268 4-5 cubic inches.

MISCELLANEOUS.

1 Chaldron makes 36 bushels, or 44 8-10 cubic feet, standard measure.

1 Chaldron makes 36 imperial bushels, or 57 25-100 cubic feet.

1 bushel of bituminous coal weighs from 74 to 80 lbs.

26 bushels make 1 ton.

1 cubic foot of anthracite coal weighs 60 to 65 lbs.

1 cubic foot of bituminous coal weighs 55 to 60 lbs.

1 cubic foot of charcoal of hard wood, weighs 18 to 19 lbs.

1 cubic foot of charcoal soft wood weighs 16 to 17 lbs.

1 cord of wood weighs from 2800 to 3400 lbs.

1 ton of timber as usually surveyed contains 50 92-100 cubic feet.

——:o:——

MEASURE OF TIME.

60 seconds make	1 minute.	m.
60 minutes make	1 hour.	h.
24 hours make	1 day.	da.
7 days make	1 week.	w.
365 1-4 days, or 52 wks.		
1 1-4 days, make	1 Julian year.	y.
12 calendar months (mo.)	1 year.	y.

Sec.	M.	H.	D.	W.	Y
60	1				
3,600	60	1			
86,400	1,440	24	1		
604,800	10,080	168	7	1	
31,557,600	525,960	8,766	365 1-4	52 5-28	1

CIRCULAR MEASURE.

60 seconds (″) make	1 minute.	′
60 minutes make	1 degree.	°
30 degrees make	1 sign.	s
12 signs or 360 degs. make the circle of zodiac.		c

″	′	°	s.	c.
60	1			
3,600	60	1		
108,000	1,800	30	1	
1,296,000	21,600	360	12	1

Minutes are designated by an accent (′.)

Seconds are designated by a double accent (″.)

Degrees are expressed by writing a ° over them as 37° for 37 degrees. Thus: 37°, 15′, 21″, 39‴, is read, 37 degrees, 15 minutes, 21 seconds and 39 thirds.

——:o:——

MENSURATION OF SURFACES.

A Surface is that which has length and breadth, without thickness.

The Area of a figure is its surface or superficial contents.

A Line is length, without breadth or thickness.

A Plane is that in which if any two points be taken the straight line that joins them will lie wholly in it.

An Angle is the inclination of opening of two lines which meet in a point.

The Vertex of an angle is the point of meeting of the lines forming the angle.

A Right Angle is an angle formed by one line falling perpendicularly on another, and it contains 90 degrees, and forms a quarter of a circle.

An Acute Angle is an angle less than a right angle or less than 90 degrees.

An Obtuse Angle is an angle greater than a right angle or more than 90 degrees.

A Triangle is a plain figure having three angles.

The Base of a triangle or other plain figure is one of its sides on which it may be supposed to stand.

The Altitude of a triangle is a line drawn from one of its angles perpendicular to its opposite side or base.

——:o:——

To find the Area of a Triangle.

RULE 1. Multiply the base by half the altitude and he product will be the area.

A Rectangle parallelogram.

A Square parallelogram.

A Rhomboid parallelogram.

A Rhombus parallelogram have all their sides equal.

To find the Area of a Parallelogram.

RULE 1. Multiply the base by the altitude and the product will be the area.

RULE 2. Add the three sides together, take half that sum and from this subtract each side separately, then multiply the half of the sum and these remainders together, and the square root of this product will be the area.

——:o:——

Trapezium. *Trapezoid.* *Irregular Polygon.*

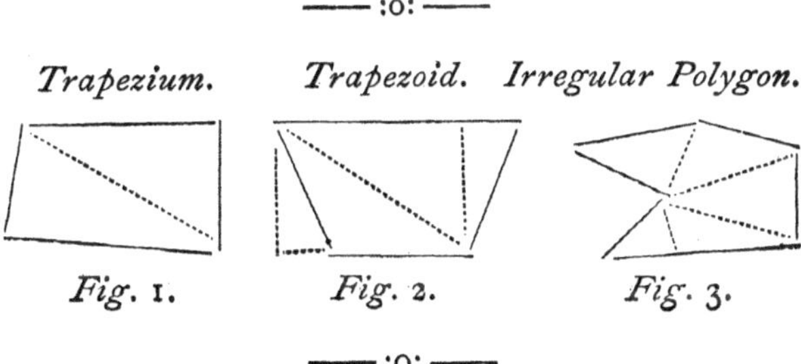

Fig. 1. *Fig.* 2. *Fig.* 3.

——:o:——

To find the Area of Figures 1, 2 and 3.

RULE—Draw diagonals to divide the figure into trapeziums and triangles as the dotted lines show, find the area of each separately and add them together and the sum of the whole will be the area.

——:o:——

To find the Circumference of a Circle.

RULE—Multiply the diameter by 3.1416 the product will be the circumference.

To find the Diameter of a Circle.

RULE—Divide the circumference by 3.1416 the product will be the diameter.

——:o:——

To find the Area of a Circle.

RULE 1. Multiply half the diameter by half of the circumference the product will be the area.

RULE 2. Multiply the square of the diameter by 7854 and the product will be the area.

——:o:——

To find the side of Square inscribed in a given Circle.

A Square is said to be inscribed in a Circle, when the vertices of its angles are in the circumference as shown by figure 4.

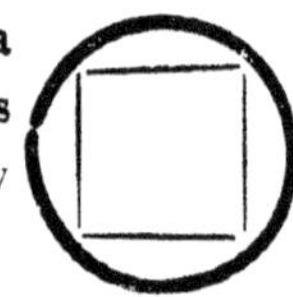

Fig. 4.

RULE—Multiply the diameter by .707106 and the product is the side of the square inscribed.

——:o:——

To find the Area of an Oval or Ellipse.

An Oval has two diameters or axes, the longer of

which is called the transverse, and the shorter the conjugate diameter.

RULE—Multiply the two diameters together, and the product by 7,854; the last product will be the area.

—— :o: ——

To find the Surface of a Sphere or Globe.

RULE—Multiply the diameter by the circumference, and the product will be the surface.

—— :o: ——

MENSURATION OF SOLIDS.

To find the Solidity or Volume of a Sphere or Globe.

RULE—Multiply the surface by $\frac{1}{6}$th of the diameter, or multiply the cube of the diameter by 523,598, and the product will be the solid contents.

—— :o: ——

To find the Solidity of a Cylinder.

RULE—Multiply the area of the end by the length of cylinder, and the product will be the solid contents.

—— :o: ——

To find the Convex Surface of a Cylinder.

RULE—Multiply the circumference by the length, the product will be the convex surface.

2

To find the Solidity of a Pyramid or a Cone.

RULE—Multiply the area of the base by one-third of its height, the product will be the solid contents.

——:o:——

To find the Surface of a Frustrum of a Pyramid or a Cone.

RULE—Add the circumference of the two ends together, and multiply this by half the slant height, then add the areas of the two ends to this product this will give the surface.

——:o:——

To find the Solidity of a Frustrum of a Cone.

RULE—Find the area of the two ends of the frustrum; multiply these two areas together and extract the square root of the product, to this root add the two areas, and multiply their sum by one-third of the height of the frustrum, the product will be the solid contents.

——:o:——

To find the Solidity of a Spheroid or Oblong Oval

RULE—Multiply the square of the shorter axis by the longer axis, and this product by .523598, which will give the solid contents.

AREAS OF CYLINDERS.

FROM 2 INCHES TO 25 INCHES IN DIAMETER.

DIAM.	AREA.	DIAM.	AREA.	DIAM.	AREA.	DIAM.	AREA.
2	3.141	7¾	47.173	13½	143.139	19¼	291.03
2⅛	3.564	7⅞	48.707	13⅝	145.802	19⅜	294.83
2¼	3.976	8	50.265	13¾	148.489	19½	298.64
2⅜	4.430	8⅛	51.848	13⅞	151.201	19⅝	302.48
2½	4.908	8¼	53.456	14	153.858	19¾	306.35
2⅝	5.411	8⅜	55.088	14⅛	156.699	19⅞	310.24
2¾	5.939	8½	56.745	14¼	159.485	20	314.16
2⅞	6.491	8⅝	58.426	14⅜	162.295	20⅛	318.09
3	7.068	8¾	60.132	14½	165.130	20¼	322.06
3⅛	7.669	8⅞	61.862	14⅝	167.980	20⅜	326.05
3¼	8.295	9	63.671	14¾	170.873	20½	330.06
3⅜	8.946	9⅛	65.396	14⅞	173.782	20⅝	334.10
3½	9.621	9¼	67.200	15	176.715	20¾	338.16
3⅝	10.320	9⅜	69.029	15⅛	179.672	20⅞	342.25
3¾	11.044	9½	70.882	15¼	182.654	21	346.36
3⅞	11.793	9⅝	72.759	15⅜	185.661	21⅛	350.49
4	12.566	9¾	74.662	15½	188.692	21¼	354.65
4⅛	13.364	9⅞	76.588	15⅝	191.748	21⅜	358.84
4¼	14.186	10	78.540	15¾	194.828	21½	363.05
4⅜	15.033	10⅛	80.515	15⅞	197 983	21⅝	367.28
4½	15.904	10¼	82.516	16	201.062	21¾	371.54
4⅝	16.800	10⅜	84.540	16⅛	204.216	21⅞	375.82
4¾	17.720	10½	86.590	16¼	207.397	22	380.13
4⅞	18.665	10⅝	88.664	16⅜	210.591	22⅛	384.46
5	19 635	10¾	89.762	16½	213.82	22¼	388.82
5⅛	20.629	10⅞	92.885	16⅝	217.07	22⅜	393.20
5¼	21.647	11	95.033	16¾	220 35	22½	397.60
5⅜	22.690	11⅛	97.203	16⅞	223.65	22⅝	402.03
5½	23.758	11¼	99.402	17	226.98	22¾	406.49
5⅝	24.850	11⅜	101.623	17⅛	230.33	22⅞	410 91
5¾	25.967	11½	103.869	17¼	233.70	23	415.47
5⅞	27.108	11⅝	106.139	17⅜	237.10	23⅛	420.00
6	28.274	11¾	108.434	17½	240.52	23¼	424.55
6⅛	29.464	11⅞	110.753	17⅝	243.97	23⅜	429.13
6¼	30.679	12	113.097	17¾	247 45	23½	433.73
6⅜	31.919	12⅛	115.466	17⅞	250.94	23⅝	438.36
6½	33.183	12¼	117.859	18	254.46	23¾	443.01
6⅝	34.471	12⅜	120.276	18⅛	258.01	23⅞	447.69
6¾	35.784	12½	122.718	18¼	261.58	24	452.39
6⅞	37.122	12⅝	125.174	18⅜	265.18	24⅛	457.11
7	38.484	12¾	127.676	18½	268.80	24¼	461.86
7⅛	39.871	12⅞	130.192	18⅝	272.44	24⅜	466.63
7¼	41.282	13	132.732	18¾	276 11	24½	471.43
7⅜	42.718	13⅛	135.297	18⅞	279.81	24⅝	476.25
7½	44.178	13¼	137.886	19	283.52	24¾	481.10
7⅝	45.663	13⅜	140.500	19⅛	287.27	24⅞	485.97

RULE.—To find the area of a Cylinder, multiply the diameter of the cylinder by the diameter in inches, and multiply the product by the decimal .7854; the product will be the area in square inches. The principle of this Rule is that for every imaginable diameter of a circle, if a square be circumscribed around it, the circle will occupy .7854 part of such square.

To get the solid contents of a cylinder, multiply its end area by the combined length of the stroke and clearance in inches; the product will be the capacity of the cylinder in cubic inches, which divided by 1728 will give the cubic feet.

——:o:——

BOILER IRON.

WEIGHT AND CUBIC INCHES PER SQUARE FOOT.

Thickness.	Cubic inches,	Weight.
$\frac{1}{8}$	$17\frac{1}{2}$	5 lbs.
$\frac{3}{16}$	$26\frac{1}{4}$	$7\frac{1}{2}$ "
$\frac{1}{4}$	35	10 "
$\frac{5}{16}$	$43\frac{3}{4}$	$12\frac{1}{2}$ "
$\frac{3}{8}$	$52\frac{1}{2}$	15 "
$\frac{7}{16}$	$61\frac{1}{4}$	17 "
$\frac{1}{2}$	70	20 "

RULE.—To get the weight of $\frac{1}{4}$ inch iron, multiply the length by the width, both in inches, and multiply the product by .7, and point off three figures for decimals; the result is the weight in pounds.

For $\frac{5}{16}$ inch iron, the weight may be first found for $\frac{1}{4}$ inch iron, and one-quarter of the sum so found may be then added to itself.

For $\frac{3}{8}$ inch iron, first find the weight for $\frac{1}{4}$ inch iron, and add half as much more.

For $\frac{1}{2}$ inch iron, multiply the length by the width, both in inches, and multiply the product by .14. Point off two figures for decimals, and the last product will be the weight in pounds.

No. 1 iron is $\frac{5}{16}$ of an inch thick.
No. 3 iron is $\frac{9}{32}$ of an inch thick.
No. 4 iron is $\frac{1}{4}$ of an inch thick.
No. 5 iron is $\frac{7}{32}$ of an inch thick.
No. 7 iron is $\frac{3}{16}$ of an inch thick.

——:o:——

SPEED OF PISTONS.

The speed of pistons of different engines varies in number of feet traveled per minute.

Common Rule.

Small Stationary....................	190 to 230 feet.
Large "	250 to 300 "
Sound and River Boats............	300 to 600 "
Marine Engines..................	220 to 550 "
Corliss Engines..................	400 to 500 "
Locomotive........................	400 to 650 "
And sometimes....................	1000 to 1100 "

WEIGHT OF RAILS PER MILE.

This table shows the weight in tons per mile for a single track, for the different weight of rails per yard.

WEIGHT PER YARD.	WEIGHT PER MILE.		
Pounds.	Tons.	Cwt.	Lbs.
40	70	8	
45	78	4	
50	88	18	
52	91	14	40
55	96		16
57	103	6	40
60	105	12	
64	112	12	80
70	113	4	
75	122		

——:o:——

DECIMALS OF ONE INCH.

1/16	.0625	9/16	.5625
1/8	.125	5/8	.625
3/16	.1875	11/16	.6875
1/4	.25	3/4	.75
5/16	.3125	13/16	.8125
3/8	.375	7/8	.875
7/16	.4385	15/16	.9375
1/2	.5	1	1.0

DECIMALS OF ONE FOOT.

½ inch	.0416	6½ inch	.5416
1 inch	.0833	7 inch	.5833
1½ inch	.125	7½ inch	.625
2 inch	.1667	8 inch	.6667
2½ inch	.2083	8½ inch	.7083
3 inch	.25	9 inch	.75
3½ inch	.2916	9½ inch	.7916
4 inch	.3333	10 inch	.8333
4½ inch	.375	10½ inch	.875
5 inch	.4166	11 inch	.9166
5½ inch	.4583	11½ inch	.9583
6 inch	.5	12 inch	1.

AREAS OF SAFETY VALVES.

In. Diam.	Square In.	In. Diam	Square In.	In. Diam.	Square In.
1¾	2.40	2¾	5.94	3¾	11.04
1⅞	2.76	2⅞	6.49	3⅞	11.76
2	3.14	3	7.07	4	12.57
2⅛	3.55	3⅛	7.67	4⅛	13.36
2¼	3.98	3¼	8.30	4¼	14.19
2⅜	4.43	3⅜	8.95	4⅜	15.03
2½	4.91	3½	6.62	4½	15.90
2⅝	5.42	3⅝	10.32	4⅝	16.80

In multiplying decimal numbers, allow as many places for decimals in the product as there are decimal places in the multiplier and multiplicand together.

In dividing decimal numbers, allow as many places for decimals in the quotient as, taken with those of the divisor, will together make up the number of decimal places in the dividend.

AREAS OF FLUES.

Areas of 1¾ inch Flues.			Areas of 1⅞ inch Flues.			Areas of 2 inch Flues.			Areas of 2¼ inch Flues.		
Length.		Exterior Surface	Length.		Exterior Surface.	Length.		Exterior Surface.	Length.		Exterior Surface.
Ft.	In.	Squr. Ft	Ft.	In.	Squr. Ft	Ft.	In.	Squr. Ft	Ft.	In.	Squr. Ft
9	0	4.123	9	0	4.417	9	0	4.712	9	0	5.303
9	1	4.161	9	1	4.458	9	1	4.756	9	1	5.352
9	2	4.200	9	2	4.499	9	2	4.800	9	2	5.401
9	3	4.238	9	3	4.539	9	3	4.843	9	3	5.450
9	4	4.276	9	4	4.580	9	4	4.887	9	4	5 499
9	5	4.314	9	5	4.621	9	5	4.931	9	5	5.548
9	6	4.352	9	6	4.662	9	6	4.974	9	6	5.597
9	7	4.391	9	7	4.703	9	7	5.018	9	7	5.646
9	8	4.429	9	8	4.744	9	8	5.062	9	8	5.695
9	9	4.467	9	9	4.785	9	9	5.105	9	9	5.744
9	10	4.515	9	10	4.826	9	10	5.149	9	10	5.793
9	11	4.543	9	11	4.867	9	11	5.192	9	11	5.842
10	0	4.581	10	0	4.908	10	0	5.236	10	0	5:981
10	1	4.620	10	1	4.948	10	1	5.280	10	1	5.940
10	2	4.658	10	2	4.989	10	2	5.325	10	2	5.989
10	3	4.696	10	3	5.030	10	3	5.367	10	3	6.038
10	4	4.734	10	4	5.071	10	4	5.411	10	4	6.087
10	5	4.772	10	5	5.112	10	5	5.454	10	5	6.136
10	6	4.811	10	6	5 153	10	6	5.498	10	6	6.185
10	7	4.849	10	7	5.194	10	7	5.541	10	7	6.234
10	8	4.887	10	8	5.235	10	8	5.585	10	8	6.283
10	9	4.925	10	9	5.276	10	9	5.629	10	9	6.332
10	10	4.963	10	10	5.317	10	10	5.672	10	10	6.381
10	11	5.001	10	11	5.357	10	11	5.716	10	11	6.430
11	0	5.040	11	0	5.398	11	0	5.760	11	0	6.479
11	1	5.078	11	1	5.439	11	1	5.803	11	1	6.528
11	2	5.116	11	2	5.480	11	2	5.847	11	2	6.577
11	3	5.154	11	3	5.521	11	3	5.891	11	3	6.626
11	4	5.192	11	4	5.562	11	4	5.934	11	4	6.675
11	5	5.230	11	5	5.603	11	5	5.978	11	5	6.724
11	6	5.269	11	6	5.644	11	6	6.021	11	6	6.774
11	7	5.307	11	7	5.685	11	7	6.065	11	7	6.823
11	8	5.345	11	8	5.726	11	8	6.109	11	8	6.872
11	9	5.383	11	9	5.766	11	9	6.152	11	9	6.921
11	10	5.421	11	10	5.807	11	10	6.196	11	10	6.970
11	11	5.460	11	11	5.848	11	11	6.240	11	11	7.019
12	0	5.498	12	0	5.889	12	0	6.283	12	0	7.068
12	1	5.536	12	1	5.930	12	1	6.327	12	1	7.117
12	2	5.574	12	2	5.971	12	2	6.371	12	2	7.166

The above table is designed to facilitate the calculation of the heating surface of the flues of the Locomotive Boiler, and is adapted for flues of various lengths, from 9 feet to 12 feet 2 inches long, and of various diameters: from 1¾ to 2¼ inches, being such as are used in the Locomotive.

EXAMPLE.—Required the heating surface of 150 flues, 11 inches exterior diameter; length of flues 11 feet. As we have found the length of flue (11 foot) in the first column, and opposite, in the next column to the right, we find 5.040 feet, being the area of one flue; which, being multiplied by 150, gives the total area of 756 square feet of flue-heating surface: 150 x 5.040=756 square feet.

——:o:——

RESISTANCE OF TRAINS.

The resistance of railway trains, moving at a speed of 6 or 8 miles per hour, is rated at 8 lbs. per ton. The resistance increases as the speed of the train increases, on account of the small nozzles, counter pressure in cylinders, and the atmospheric resistance. At the rate of 30 miles per hour, the resistance will be about 16 lbs. per ton. At 60 miles per hour, the resistance is more than one half the power expended, in overcoming the atmospheric resistance.

Resistance of trains on different roads, at a speed of 6 miles per hour; friction 8 lbs. per ton:

TABLE.

Grade. Feet per Mile.	Resistance in lbs. per ton, of train	Grade. Feet per mile.	Resistance in lbs. per ton, of train.	Grade. Feet per mile.	Resistance per lb. per ton, of train.
Level.	8.	70 Feet.	34.5	140 Feet.	61.
5 Feet.	9.9	75 "	36.4	145 "	62.9
10 "	11.8	80 "	38.3	150 "	64.8
15 "	13.7	85 "	40.2	155 "	66.6
20 "	15.6	90 "	42.1	160 "	68 2
25 "	17.5	95 "	44.	165 "	70.5
30 "	19.4	100 "	45.9	170 "	72.3
35 "	21.2	105 "	47.7	175 "	74.2
40 "	23.1	110 "	49.6	180 "	76.
45 "	25.	115 "	51.5	185 "	78.1
50 "	26.9	120 "	53.4	190 "	79.9
55 "	28.8	125 "	55.3	195 "	81.8
60 "	30.7	130 "	57.	200 "	83.7
65 "	32.6	135 "	59.1		

RULE.—To find the resistance of a train, on any grade, multiply the rise, in feet, per mile, by .3787, and point off four decimals; the product is the resistance of one ton, 2,000 lbs.

What is the resistance of a freight train of 250 tons, on a 70 feet grade?

EXAMPLE.—250 x 345=8,625 lbs.

TABLE.

Showing the temperature of steam, at different pressures, from 1 lb. per square inch, to 200 lbs.; and the quantity of steam produced from a cubic inch of water, according to pressure:

Pressure in lbs., Per square inch.	Corresponding temperature, by Fahrenheit's thermometer.	Cubic inches of steam from a cubic inch of water, according to pressure.	Pressure in lbs., Per square inch.	Corresponding temperature, by Fahrenheit's thermometer.	Cubic inches of steam from a cubic inch of water, according to pressure.
1	102.9	20954	26	243.0	1005
2	126.1	10907	27	245.1	971
3	141.0	7455	28	247.2	939
4	152.3	5695	29	249.2	909
5	161.4	4624	30	251.2	882
6	169.2	3901	31	253.1	855
7	176.0	3380	32	255.0	831
8	182.0	2985	33	256.8	808
9	187.4	2676	34	258.6	786
10	192.4	2427	35	260.3	765
11	197.0	2222	36	262.0	746
12	201.3	2050	37	263.7	727
13	205.3	1903	38	265.3	710
14	209.0	1777	39	266.9	693
15	213.0	1669	40	268.4	677
16	216.4	1572	41	269.9	662
17	219.6	1487	42	271.4	647
18	222.6	1410	43	272.9	634
19	225.6	1342	44	274.3	620
20	228.3	1280	45	275.7	608
21	231.0	1224	46	277.1	596
22	233.6	1172	47	278.4	584
23	236.1	1125	48	279.7	573
24	238.4	1082	49	281.0	562
25	240.7	1042	50	282.3	552

TABLE.

Pressure in lbs., Per square inch.	Corresponding temperature, by Fahrenheit's thermometer.	Cubic inches of steam from a cubic inch of water, according to pressure.	Pressure in lbs., Per square inch.	Corresponding temperature, by Fahrenheit's thermometer.	Cubic inches of steam from a cubic inch of water, according to pressure.
51	283.6	542	81	314.3	355
52	284.8	532	82	315.2	351
53	286.0	523	83	316.1	348
54	287.2	514	84	316.9	344
55	288.4	506	85	317.8	340
56	289.6	498	86	318.6	337
57	290.7	490	87	319.4	333
58	291.9	482	88	320 3	330
59	293.0	474	89	321.1	326
60	294.1	467	90	321.9	323
61	294.9	460	91	322.7	320
62	295.9	453	92	323.5	317
63	297.0	447	93	324.3	313
64	298.1	440	94	325.0	310
65	299.1	434	95	325.8	307
66	300.1	428	96	326.6	305
67	301.2	422	97	327.3	302
68	302.2	417	98	328.1	299
69	303.2	411	99	328.8	296
70	304.2	406	100	329.6	293
71	305.1	401	110	339.2	271
72	306.1	396	120	345.8	251
73	307.1	391	130	352.1	233
74	308.0	386	140	357.9	218
75	308.9	381	150	363.4	205
76	309.9	377	160	368.7	193
77	310.8	372	170	373.6	183
78	311.7	368	180	378 4	174
79	312.6	364	190	382.9	166
80	313.5	359	200	387.3	158

TABLE OF TIME.

This table gives the number of revolutions that are made by the driving wheels of different sizes, (from 4 feet to 7 feet in diameter), per minute, at different speeds, from 5 to 60 miles per hour:

Diameter of Driving Wheels.		Speed per Hour, in Miles.											
		5	10	15	20	25	30	35	40	45	50	55	60
		Revolutions per Minute.											
Feet.	Inches.												
4	0	35	70	105	140	175	210	245	280	315	350	365	420
4	3	33	66	99	132	165	194	231	264	297	330	362	395
4	6	31	62	93	124	156	186	217	249	280	311	342	373
4	9	29½	59	88	118	147	177	203	236	265	295	324	354
5	0	28	56	84	112	140	168	196	224	252	280	308	336
5	3	26⅔	53	80	107	133	160	187	213	240	267	293	320
5	6	25½	51	76	102	127	153	178	204	229	255	280	306
5	9	24⅓	48	73	97	122	146	170	195	219	243	267	292
6	0	23⅓	46	70	93	117	140	163	186	210	233	255	280
6	3	22½	45	67	89	112	134	156	178	201	223	244	268
6	6	21½	43	64	86	108	129	151	172	194	216	237	259
6	9	20¼	40	61	81	111	121	142	164	182	222	223	243
7	0	20	40	60	80	100	120	140	160	180	200	220	240

Steam used at one revolution, in both cylinders of a Locomotive:

Cylinder.	Cubic feet.	Cylinder.	Cubic feet.	Cylinder.	Cubic feet.
11 x16	3.5197	14 x18	6.4140	16½x22	10.8890
11 x20	4.3996	14 x20	7 1270	17 x20	10.5083
11½x16	3.8470	15 x18	7.3631	17 x22	11.5591
11¾x20	5.0200	15 x20	8.1812	17 x24	12.6099
12 x16	4.1890	15 x22	8.9993	18 x20	11.7809
12 x18	4.7123	15 x24	9.8174	18 x22	12.9590
12 x20	5.2360	15½x22	9.6090	18 x24	14.1371
12¼x16	4.3550	16 x18	8.3775	19 x22	14.1490
12¾x16	4.7280	16 x20	9.3084	20 x22	15.9988
13 x20	6.1460	16 x22	10 2392	16 x26	12.1009
13½x20	6.6268	16 x24	11.1700	15½x26	11.1751

RESISTANCE OF TRAINS.

The following formulas are by D. K. CLARK, and are for the broad gauge. In this country some addition would be required for the inferior condition and sharper curvature of our roads. Actual resistance can only be ascertained by experiment; but it is probable that the following rules would give a result from 20 to 30 per cent. too low for the majority of our roads, as the rules were made upon very elaborate tests, on an excellent road, and under favorable circumstances.

RULE I.—To find the total resistance of an engine, tender and train, at a given speed, square the speed in miles per hour, divide it by 171, and add 8 to the quotient; the result is the total resistance at the rails, in pounds, per ton weight.

RULE II.—To find the resistance of the train alone, at a given speed, square the speed in miles, per hour, divide it by 240, and add 6 to the quotient; the result is the resistance at the rails, in pounds, per ton weight.

RULE III.· To find the resistance of the engine and tender alone, with a given train, at a given speed,

First. Find the resistance, as carriages, by Rule II.

Second. Square the speed, and divide it by 600, and add 2 to the quotient; multiply the sum thus found, by the total weight of engine, tender, and train, and divide by the weight of the engine and tender; the quotient expresses the total machinery friction.

Third. Add together the two results thus obtained,

the sum is the whole resistance at the rails, in pounds, per ton weight.

At slow speeds the principal resistance is friction, and this element is constant at all velocities; the additional resistance being dependant on concussions, the atmospheres, etc. Friction is a constant quantity of about 8 pounds per ton, at all speeds. This element varies with the condition of the cars. It would be said that an engine works harder in starting at a slow speed, than in running at a high speed. This is only apparently so, as the greater effort of the engine, in starting, is in increasing the speed, and not in maintaining it at any fixed point. In increasing the speed, the inertia of the train is to be overcome, of course. An engine, while it may not be able to make time with a heavy train, may yet be able to haul it slowly. The actual resistance of motion increases rapidly with the speed, especially where the road is not in good order.

There are several reasons why the power of the engine diminishes at high speeds. One is the wire-drawing of steam through small and slow-opening ports, and small exhaust nozzles. Another is, that in working the engine, cutting off the steam close, which is done on high speeds, the power being thereby diminished, although the work done by a given amount of steam is increased. Another is the greater compression, which is a counterforce to the power.

PRESSURE ON BOILERS.

The question has been asked what part of the boiler has the greatest pressure, when under steam. I have tested a boiler, by attaching steam guages to various parts: mud drum, bottom of leg, side and top, of boiler. Results, when there is no steam in the boiler; the guages attached to the lower parts of the boiler, show the weight of water; after steam has been raised, there is no difference; guages showing the same, up to 150 pounds pressure per square inch.

——:o:——

RADIUS OF CURVES.

For calculating the radius of a curve, when the angle of deflection and chord is given. Railroad curves are always laid off with chords of 100 feet; and we often find, when speaking of curves, the angle of deflection is merely given. Now, to find the radius: 5,730 feet is a common radius, which is equal to a deflection of 1°.

RULE.—Divide the number of degrees deflected into 5,370; the product will be the radius of the curve; or divide the radius into 5,730, the product will be the degrees of the curve.

EXAMPLE.—We have a curve with a deflection of 8°, and the chord of 100 feet:

8)5,730
  $716\frac{1}{4}$ feet radius of curve.

EXPLANATION OF TIME TABLE.

The Diagram on opposite page, shows how time-tables are prepared for running trains on railroads; the stations being laid off to a scale of miles one way, and the time in hours and minutes the other way. The broken lines show the time trains stop at stations, and passing-points. When making out a time-table, if the road be 175 miles long, lay out 175 lines, equal distance apart; then lay out the distance between stations, by counting each line for one mile, dividing up between lines for ½ and ¼ miles when required, placing the name of station upon the line, and distance in miles between stations, as shown in diagram, it being necessary only to draw lines across the table that the names of stations come upon.

Lay out the other way in hours and minutes for 24 hours. All the first-class trains are to be started first, running in both directions, giving speed per hour and time stopping at stations. Then the second-class trains, showing speed and time arriving in advance of first-class trains' time, giving proper clearance which is generally about 10 minutes at passing-points.

Example: In referring to time-table, we find that the Express leaves Newark 6.50 a. m., arriving at Ross 7.57 a. m., speed 30 miles per hour, passing the way Passenger at Ross, which left Newark 6.20 a. m., arriving 7.54 a. m., speed 23 miles per hour, Express arrives at Paterson 8.40 a. m.; way Passenger arrives 9.20 a. m.

We also find a Freight and a Passenger train which left Paterson running from opposite direction, which have arrived at Ross; Freight 11 minutes, Passenger 3 minutes before the Express' arriving time, so as to take the side track for the Express. Trains of the same class have the same arriving time which can be seen by inspecting the table.

Double track roads require 2 diagrams, one for each track to make out a time table, as the trains all run one way on each track, there being no meeting of trains. For want of space this diagram was laid out in hours and ten minutes instead of hours and minutes.

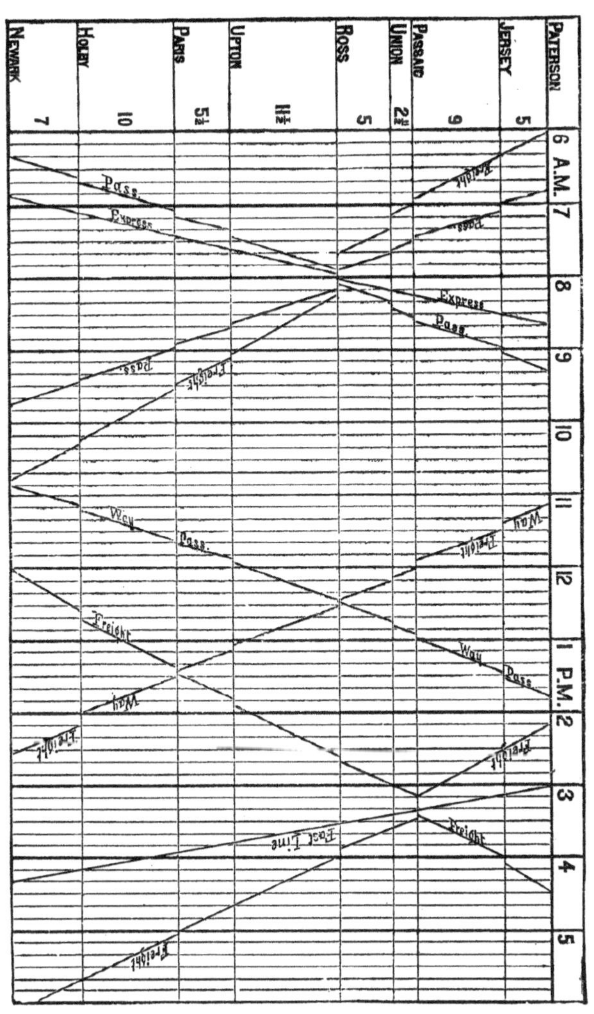
Paterson
Jersey 5
Passaic 9
Union 2½
Ross 5
Upton 11½
Paris 5½
Holby 10
Newark 7
6 A.M.
7
8
9
10
11
12
1 P.M.
2
3
4
5
Pass.
Express
Freight
Way
Fast Line

BRASS, OR COMPOSITION.

Babbit Metal.—2 lbs. copper, 4 lbs. antimony, and 41 lbs. tin.

Muntz Metal.—2 lbs. of zinc and 3 lbs. of copper.

Locomotive Brasses.—6½ to 7lbs. of copper, to 1 lb. of tin.

Car Brasses.—5 lbs. of copper to 1 lb. of tin.

Common Yellow Brass.—2 lbs. of copper, 1 lb of zinc.

Good gold color Brass,—8 lbs. copper, 1 lb. of tin, and 2½ oz. zinc.

Very Tough Brass.—8½ lbs. of copper, 1 lb. of tin.

Large Bell Metal.—4 lbs. of copper, 19 oz. of tin, 1¼ oz. of zinc.

Tombar, or Red Brass.—8 lbs. copper, 1 lb. zinc.

White Copper.—16 lbs. of copper, 1 lb. of arsenic.

Brazing Solder, very hard.—3 lbs. of copper, 1 lb. of tin. *Hard.*—7 lbs. of common yellow brass, 1 lb. zinc. *Soft.*—5½ lbs. eommon yellow brass, 1 lb. of tin, and 1 lb. of zinc.

Plumbers' Solder.—1 lb. of tin, 1 lb. of lead.

Tinmans' Solder.—1 lb. of tin, 2 lbs. of lead.

Pewter Solder.—2 lbs. of tin, 1 lb. of lead.

Common Pewter.—4 lbs. of tin, 1 lb. of lead.

A Metal that Expands in Cooling.—9 lbs. of lead, 2 lbs. of antimony, and 1 lb. of bismuth.

The copper must be melted first. Mix or add the other metals, just before casting. Add the antimony, with small portions of tin; stir well before casting.

The metal should be strewn over with charcoal, to prevent oxidation.

——:o:——

CASE-HARDENING.

As a general rule, the Locomotive Engine has the links, and all the working parts belonging to the link and valve motion, case-hardened; also the slides and crank pins, when not made of steel. There are several methods of case-hardening. The quality and depth of steel required depends on the material used, the uniformity of the heat, and the time of remaining in the furnace. The best method consists in placing the articles to be operated upon in an iron box made for the purpose, with a layer of charred leather and bone dust; the articles to be so placed as not to touch each other, and to be well covered with the bone dust and charred leather, the lid of the box to be tightly fitted. The joints and lid of box must be luted with clay, so as to be air-tight. After the box has been in the furnace the required time, the contents must be speedily taken out of the box and suddenly immersed in cold water. The time of remaining in the furnace depends on the size of the articles to be hardened. For small work, from ten to twelve hours will answer; for links and slides, from twenty-six to twenty-eight hours, to get a good depth of hardening. When not particular to the depth, it can be done with Prussiate of potash, by heating the iron to a red heat, and coating it over with potash, and placing it in the fire again, a few minutes, then immersed in water.

The temper may be taken out of a case-hardened piece of iron, so as to turn or file, by heating; the piece to be annealed to a dark red, and allowing it to cool in the open air. The hardening can be regained by re-heating the iron to a red heat, and immersing it in salt water; it will receive all of its previous hardness.

——:o:——

SHRINKAGE FOR STEEL TIRES.

There are many different opinions in regard to setting tires, as regards the shrinkage. The results from the following rules, have given good satisfaction:

$\frac{1}{30}$ of an inch for a 3-foot 6-inch wheel.
$\frac{1}{25}$ of an inch for a 4-foot wheel.
$\frac{1}{23}$ of an inch for a 4-foot 6-inch wheel.
$\frac{1}{20}$ of an inch for a 5-foot wheel.
$\frac{1}{16}$ of an inch for a 5-foot 6-inch wheel.
$\frac{1}{13}$ of an inch for a 6-foot wheel.

——:o:——

COUNTERBALANCING DRIVING-WHEELS.

The reciprocating, as well as the revolving parts, are to be counterbalanced.

All the revolving parts, attached to each crank-pin, must be counterbalanced in the wheel to which they are attached.

The reciprocating parts are to be equally divided, according to the number of driving-wheels.

For an outside-cylinder, four-wheel, connected-engine, proceed as follows:—For each side get the weight of piston, piston-rod, cross-head, pump-plunger, and cross-head end of main rod; call these the reciprocating parts. Then get the weight of the crank-pin, the crank-pin boss, the back end of main rod, and one-half the weight of the parallel rod; to this add one-half of the above reciprocating weight. The product will be the weight to be counterbalanced in the forward, or main driving-wheel.

For the back driving-wheel, get the weight of its caank-pin, the crank-pin boss, and one-half of the parallel rod; to this add the remaining half of the reciprocating weight, the product will be the weight to be counterbalanced in the back wheel.

For an inside-cylinder, four-wheel, connected-engine, proceed the same as before, to get the weight of the reciprocating parts; then get the weight of the crank end of main rod, crank-wrist, and one crank-throw; deduct one-quarter of their total weight, and add the whole weight of the outside crank-pin, crank-pin boss, and one-half of parallel rod; to this add one-half of the reciprocating weight. The product will be the weight; to be counterbalanced in the forward or main driving-wheel.

For the back wheel, take the revolving weight attached to the crank-pin, and one-half of the reciprocating weight, the same as for an outside-cylinder, or outside-connected engine, as it is termed.

Next find the centre of gravity of the counter-weight to be used; after the shape is fixed upon, cut out a wooden template, and find its centre of gravity, by suspending it freely, first from one corner, and dropping a plumb-line from the point of suspension, and marking its position, and then repeating the operation from another corner, and noting the point of intersection of the line with the first position, which will be the centre of gravity.

Now, having determined the position which the counter-weight will occupy, its exact weight may be determined by multiplying the weight respectively to be balanced in each wheel, by the length of the crank, and divide the product by the distance of the centre of gravity from the centre of the axle; the product is the weight of counterbalance for each wheel.

If three or more counter-weights are to be used together, in the same wheel, a common centre of gravity must be found for all, by drawing an arc through the centre of gravity of the balances, and connecting the centres of gravity of the two outside balances by a straight line; then take from the middle of straight line one-third of the distance between the straight line and the curved line which cuts through the centres, which will be the common centre of gravity.

When very small wheels are used, as is commonly the case with heavy engines of the Mogul and consolidation patterns, it is often difficult to get room for counterbalances of the requisite weight in each wheel; under these circumstances the weight is divided equally for each wheel, or attached, as circumstances will admit.

Passenger engines, with large wheels, are often counterbalanced by casting the spokes and rim of the wheel hollow, and filling them with lead.

——:o:——

POWER OF THE LOCOMOTIVE.

The adhesive power of the Locomotive is the power of the engine, derived from the weight on its driving-wheels; therefore, the force which propels the train upon the rail, is the adhesion between the tires of the driving-wheels and the rails. If the friction between these two be less than the friction between the wheels on the train and the rails, the driving-wheels will slip and turn, without advancing on the rail. An engine, with six-driving-wheels connected, or ten-wheel engine, as it is termed, has a much larger proportion of the whole weight of the engine brought into action on the rails for producing adhesion, than is the case with the four driving wheel connected, or eight-wheel engine, as it is termed, as the truck of the eight-wheel engine carries a little over one-third of the whole weight of engine on the truck, which is unavoidable; while the ten-wheel, or six-wheel connected engine only carries one-fifth of its actual weight on the engine truck, and a larger proportion of the whole weight is made available, and the power increased. If the pressure of steam in the boiler be increased to equal the additional adhesion of engine, the adhesion of the eight-wheel, or four-wheel connected-engine is overcome, generally, with 130 lbs. pressure of steam per square ineh. There is another consideration; this greater weight of the six-wheel connected engine on the rails, produces greater friction to be overcome by the cylinders; the greater, therefore, the proportion of power absorbed, and greater the wear and tear of the parts of the engine and the rails.

The four-wheel switch engine, without a truck, has the total weight of the engine on the driving-wheels; therefore a switch engine, weighing 20 tons, will have same power as a 30-ton eight-wheel engine, the weight on driving-wheels of both engines will be the same.

The tractive force of the Locomotive is the power of the engine, derived from the pressure of steam on the piston, applied to the crank and diameter of wheel.

The power of the Locomotive is measured by the moving force at the tread of the tires, and is called the tractive force; and equals the load the Locomotive could raise out of a pit, by means of a belt passing over a pully, and attached to the tread or face of one of the driving-wheels.

Rule to Calculate the Horse Power of the Locomotive Engine.

Multiply the area of piston by the pressure per square inch of steam used, which will be about $\frac{2}{3}$ of the pressure indicated by the steam guage; the one-third being deducted for the effects of early exhaust, compression, and condensation, as steam loses pressure directly as it expands. Multiply the last product by the number of revolutions per minute; multiply this by twice the length of stroke, in feet; divide the last product by 33.000, the result will be the power of one cylinder, which multiplied by 2, will give the power of both cylinders, and will be the horse power of the Locomotive.

EXAMPLE.—Area of cylinder 200 inches; pressure per square inch, 80 lbs. x 200=16,000 lbs. Driving-wheel 5 feet diameter, 15 miles per hour, gives 84 turns per minute, 84 x 16,000=1,344,000 foot-pounds. Stroke 2 feet x 2=4 x 1,344,000=5,376,000 foot-pounds ÷33,000=162$\frac{10}{11}$ horse power. This being one cylinder, x 2=325$\frac{9}{11}$ horse power of the Locomotive.

200 inches area of cylinder.
80 lbs. pressure per square inch.

16,000 total pressure.
84 revolutions per minute.

64,000
128,000

1,344,000 foot-pounds.
4 feet, being twice the length of stroke.

33,000)5,376,000 foot-pounds.
162 $\frac{30}{33}$ power of one cylinder.
2 cylinders.

325 $\frac{9}{11}$ horse power of Locomotive.

——:o:——

For Calculating the Tractive Power of the Locomotive.

RULE 1st.—Multiply the diameter of the cylinder in inches, by itself; multiply the product by the working or average pressure in the cylinder, in pounds per square inch. Multiply this product by length of stroke, in inches, and divide the last product by the diameter of the wheel, in inches, the quotient will be the tractive power.

RULE 2d.—The power of the Locomotive may be roughly computed by calling it equal to $\frac{1}{6}$th of the total weight on the driving-wheels, When the rails are dry, and in good condition, the insistant weight is usually regarded as a safe basis for ordinary calculation; hence $\frac{1}{6}$th of the weight upon the driving-wheels of a Locomotive is called its tractive power.

Example.—Required to find the tractive power of a Locomotive, when total weight on drivers is 20 tons.

One ton, 2,000 lbs. x 20=40,000 lbs. $\div$6=6,666$\frac{2}{3}$ tractive power.

One ton,	2,000	lbs.
Weight on drivers,	20	tons.
	6)40,000	lbs. weight on drivers.
	6,666$\frac{2}{3}$	lbs., $\frac{1}{6}$th of weight on

drivers or tractive power, that is: this Locomotive will draw, when the rails are in good condition, 6,666 lbs; and this load drawn is called the tractive power, or the power of the Locomotive.

——:o:——

Friction of Cars.

This term signifies the power required to draw a car on a level road, on a smooth rail. It is usually estimated that 8 lbs. is sufficient to draw 1 ton. A spring balance would be extended to 8 lbs. for every ton drawn in a car; thus, if a car contained 2 tons, the spring balance would indicate 16 pounds over and above the weight required to draw the empty car.

The reader will observe that the tractive power is expressed in pounds, the same as the friction, so that one can be converted into the other.

EXAMPLE.—Required the friction of a train of 40 cars, weight 20 tons to the car: 40 cars x 20 tons= 800 tons x 8 lbs., 6,400 lbs. of friction, or tractive power required to draw this train.

40 cars.
20 tons.
———
800 tons.
8 lbs. per car.
———
6,400 lbs. of friction.

——:o:——

Horse Power per Hour.

When using high-pressure steam, for every cubic foot of water used, when the engine is in good order, and using dry steam, may be considered one-horse power; therefore, when using a tender containing 1,800 gallons of water, which is equal to 240 cubic feet in one hour, would be exerting 240-horse power per hour.

——:o:——

DIMENSIONS OF PARTS OF LOCOMOTIVE.

To find the inside diameter of a Locomotive boiler.

RULE.—Multiply the diameter of the cylinder in inches, by 2.98; the product will be the diameter of the boiler in inches.

EXAMPLE.—Required the inside diameter of a Locomotive boiler, the diameter of cylinder being 16 inches: 16 x 2.98=$47\frac{68}{100}$ inches.

—— :o: ——

Length of Boilers.

The length of Locomotive boilers is from 18 feet to 21 feet; length of flues generally from 11 feet to 11 feet 2 or 3 inches, $1\frac{3}{4}$ inches inside diameter.

—— :o: ——

Diameter of Steam Dome.

When using one dome it is necessary to have it large enough to prevent the raising of water; the diameter or height may vary, according to circumstances.

RULE.—For a 16-inch cylinder the dome will be 26 inches in diameter, and 30 inches high, omitting the dome cover; this size dome would answer for either a 15 or 17-inch cylinder.

—— :o: ——

Area of Fire Grate.

To find the area of the fire grate of a Locomotive boiler:

RULE.—Multiply the diameter of the cylinder by 87; the product will be th[illegible] in square feet.

EXAMPLE.—To find the area of the fire grate surface of a Locomotive boiler, the cylinder being 16 inches in diameter: 16 x .87=$13\frac{92}{100}$ square feet of grate surface.

——:o:——

Area of Heating Surface.

To find the area of effective heating surface of a Locomotive boiler:

RULE.—Multiply the diameter of the cylinder by its diameter, and multiply the product by 7; divide the last product by 2; the quotient will be the area of effective heating surface, in square feet.

EXAMPLE.—To find the effective heating surface, the cylinder being 16 inches in diameter: 16 x 16= 256 x 7=1,792÷2=896 square feet.

——:o:——

Safety Valve.

In calculating the safety-valve, it does not require much exactness; all that is necessary is to have it large enough to free the boiler from its surplus steam, when the steam is shut off from the cylinders.

RULE.—One square inch of area of safety valve to 1 square foot of area of fire grate surface, will fill the demand. In all cases this proportion gives the largest area of safety valves in use on Locomotives.

The Locomotive generally has two safety-valves, each valve having half the area of that of a single valve.

Safety-Valve Lever.

To find the length of a safety-valve lever, when the spring balance is used:

RULE.—Multiply the area of the valve in square inches, by 100 lbs. pressure per square inch; divide the product by 56 lbs., and multiply the last product by the distance between the fulcrum and valve; the quotient will be the length of safety-valve lever.

EXAMPLE.—To find the length of safety-valve lever, the area of valve being 6 inches:

Area of valve,........	6		inches.
Lbs. press. per sq'r in.	100		
Total pressure.....	56)600	($10\frac{5}{7}$	
Weight,...........	56	3	in. dist. between fulcrum and valve
	40	$32\frac{1}{5}$	in., total length of lever.

56 lbs. on the end of a lever equals 100 lbs. indicated on spring balance; 28 lbs. on end of lever will indicate 50 lbs. on spring balance; 14 lbs. on end of lever will indicate 25 lbs. on spring balance, etc.

——:o:——

How to Weigh a Safety-Valve.

Fasten an upright piece on each of the two sides of the frame of a common platform scales; to fasten a piece of plank at each end, so as to form a bridge across the scales without interfering with the platform of the scales; screw the stem of the fulcrum into the top of this plank; place the valve upon the platform of the scales, and let the lever rest upon the top of the valve, at the same distance from the joint that it is fixed at when upon the engine; then multiply the area of the valve, in square inches, by the pressure required, the spring balance being attached to the end of the lever, and fastened at its other end, the same as it is attached upon the boiler; we can now set the weight of the platform scales to the number of pounds equal to the product already obtained; and the tension of the spring balance regulated by its nut and screw, which is just sufficient to balance the scale-beam, will show the point at which the spring balance will hold the safety-valve to that pressure.

——:o:——

Cubical contents of water in a Locomotive Boiler.

To find the cubical contents of water in the boiler, when having 3 guages of water:

RULE.—Multiply the diameter of the cylinder, in inches, by its diameter; multiply the product by 9, and divide the last product by 18; the quotient will be the cubical contents of the water in the boiler, in cubic feet.

EXAMPLE.—To find the cubical contents of water in a boiler of a Locomotive, the diameter of cylinder being 16 inches: 16 x 16=256 x 9=2,304÷18=128 cubic feet of water, or about 960 gallons.

Feed Pumps for a Locomotive.

A Locomotive has two pumps, or one pump and one injector. A great many roads have adopted the rule of using two pumps and one injector, which is a decided improvement.

Either pump should be capable of keeping up the supply of water at all times. The pump plungers of the Locomotive are worked in several ways; generally they are full-stroke pumps, the plunger being attached to the cross-head, and has the same stroke as the piston.

RULE.—The diameter for a full-stroke pump is $\frac{1}{8}$ to the inch of the diameter of the cylinder. Half-stroke pumps will be twice the area of the full-stroke pump.

To find the diameter of a full-stroke pump-plunger, divide the diameter of the cylinder in inches, by 8; the product will be the diameter of the plunger.

EXAMPLE.—To find the diameter of a pump-plunger, for a Locomotive whose cylinder is 16 inches in diameter: $16 \div 8 = 2$ inch diameter.

——:o:——

Feed Pipes of the Locomotive.

The feed-pipe of the Locomotive is not particular to size, so long as it is large enough. General practice gives from one-quarter to a half inch larger in diameter than the pump-plunger, so as to give full supply to the pump.

Diameter of Steam-Pipe.

To find the diameter of a steam-pipe for a Locomotive:

RULE.—Multiply the diameter of the cylinder, in inches, by its diameter; multiply the product by .03; the product will be the diameter of the steam-pipe, in inches.

EXAMPLE.—To find the diameter of steam-pipe of the Locomotive, the cylinder being 16 inches in diameter: 16 x 16=256 x .03=7.68 inches diameter.

——:o:——

Throw of Eccentric.

How to get the throw of eccentric, or travel of valve.

RULE.—It is found by adding together the width of both steam-ports, and the lap on both ends of the valve; this product will give the exact opening of steam-port, one-half inch more being added to the above product so that the edges of the valve will travel about a quarter of an inch beyond the inside edge of steam-port, on the bridge, to insure a full opening of port, when the joints have become worn.

EXAMPLE.

Width of front port....	1¼	inch.
Width of back port....	1¼	inch.
Lap of front end......	1	inch.
Lap of back end......	1	inch.
For wear of joints.....	½	inch.
Total........	5	inches travel of valve.

Diameter of Branch Pipe.

To find the diameter of the branch-pipe of the Locomotive.

RULE.—Multiply the diameter of cylinder, in inch es, by its diameter; multiply the product by .021, the quotient is the diameter of the branch-pipe, in inches.

EXAMPLE.—To find the diameter of the branch-pipe for a Locomotive, when the cylinder is 16 inches in diameter: 16 x 16=256 x .021=5$\frac{37}{100}$ inches in diameter.

——:o:——

Area of Steam Port.

The area of steam-port of the Locomotive cylinder is generally about $\frac{1}{11}$ of the area of the cylinder; the length of ports varies, as well as the width, according to the designers' ideas. General practice gives length of steam-port one inch less than the diameter of cylinder, and about 1$\frac{1}{4}$ inches wide.

RULE.—To find the area of a steam-port for a Locomotive cylinder, multiply the diameter of the cylinder, in inches, by its diameter, then multiply the product by .074; the product given will be the area in square inches. This is the simplest rule, and does not require to have the area of cylinder.

EXAMPLE.—To find the area of steam-port, when the cylinder is 16 inches in diameter: 16 x 16=256 x .074=18$\frac{94}{100}$ square inches.

Area of Exhaust Port.

To find the area of exhaust-port, the exhaust-port is required to be twice the area of the steam-port; the length of exhaust-port will be the same as the steam-port.

RULE.—Multiply the diameter of cylinder, in inches, by its diameter; multiply the product by .148; the product will be the area in square inches.

EXAMPLE.—To find the area of an exhaust-port, the cylinder being 16 inches in diameter: 16 x 16=256 x .148=$37\frac{88}{100}$ square inches.

——:o:——

Thickness of Bridges between ports.

Width of bridges, between steam and exhaust-ports, vary in thickness, from $\frac{3}{4}$ of an inch to $1\frac{1}{2}$ inch; general practice gives $1\frac{1}{8}$ to $1\frac{1}{4}$ inches.

——:o:——

Diameter of Piston Rod.

RULE.—To find the diameter of a piston-rod for a Locomotive, divide the diameter of the cylinder, in inches, by 6; the product will be the diameter of the piston-rod, in inches.

EXAMPLE.—The diameter of the cylinder being 16 inches: 16÷6=$2\frac{4}{6}$ inches in diameter.

Thickness of Piston.

RULE.—To find the thickness of piston for a Locomotive, multiply the diameter of cylinder by 2; divide the product by 8; this product will be the thickness of the piston, in inches.

EXAMPLE.—The diameter of cylinder being 16 inches 16 x 2=32 ÷8=4 inches, thickness of piston.

——:o:——

Diameter of Crank-Pin.

To find the diameter of the crank-pin of a Locomotive.

RULE.—Multiply the diameter of the cylinder, in inches, by its diameter, and divide the product by 64; the product will be the diameter, in inches.

EXAMPLE.—To find the diameter of crank-pin for a Locomotive, when the cylinder is 16 inches in diameter: 16 x 16=256÷64=4 inches.

The width of a crank-pin journal should be the same as the diameter.

——:o:——

Cross-Head Wrist-Pin.

RULE.—To find the diameter of the wrist-pin of a Locomotive, multiply the diameter of the cylinder, in inches, by its diameter, and divide the product by 72; the product will be the diameter, in inches.

EXAMPLE.—Diameter of cylinder being 16 inches? 16 x 16=256 ÷72=3½ inches.

Smoke-Stack or Chimney.

The smoke-stack of the Locomotive varies in size. Practice has shown that the stack made the same diameter, or one inch less than the diameter of the cylinder, gives the best results. Height of stack not to exceed 14 feet 3 inches from the rail.

——:o:——

Safety, or Fusible Plug.

The safety, or fusible plug, is a brass bolt 1½ inches in diameter, and 2 inches long, with a hole drilled and tapped through it, and filled with lead, and is located about in the centre of the crown-sheet in the furnace, and screwed about ⅝ of an inch through the sheet; the lead will melt out of this plug if the boiler becomes short of water; and gives notice of danger. The lead should be removed every six months, as the plug will corrode over on the end with sediment from the water, and prevent it from giving an alarm.

Built at Rogers' Locomotive Works, Paterson. N. J.

Cylinder 16x24 inches.

Weight of Engine empty, on truck	22,000 pounds.
Weight on driving-wheels	36,050 pounds.
Total weight of empty Engine	58,050 pounds.
Weight of Engine, with two guages of water, on truck	23,394 pounds.
" " " " " on driving-wheels	41,576 pounds.
Total weight of Engine	64,970 pounds.
Weight of tender, empty	20,310 pounds.
" " with water	36,690 pounds.
" " with water and coal	45,280 pounds.

Tender holds 2,047 gallons of water, and 8,590 pounds of coal. Water in boiler, 865 gallons.

IMPORTANT DIMENSIONS OF A LOCOMOTIVE ENGINE.

Such as are in general use, for 18 x 20, 17 x 22, 16 x 24, four-wheel connected-engines.

One inch in bore, or two inches in stroke, are classed as one size of a Locomotive.

Diameter of cylinder............	16	inches.
Length of stroke................	20, 22, 24	"
Steam ports; length of port 1 inch less than bore of cylinder....	1¼ x 15	"
Exhaust ports; length of port 1 inch less than bore of cylinder	2½ x 15	"
Outside lap....................	13/16	"
Inside lap.....................	1/16	"
Throw of eccentric.............	5	"
Lead, in full stroke..............	1/16	"
Horizontal distance from centre of axle to centre of rocker......	5 feet 5½	"
Centre of rocker above centre line of engine....................	7¾	"
Length of rocker arms..........	9	"
Radius of centre of link.........	5 feet 1⅜	"
Knuckle-joint centres, back of centre line of link, toward axle..	2½	"
Distance between knuckle-joint centres......................	13	"
Length of eccentric-rods, from centre of eccentric-strap to centre of knuckle-joints.............	2 15/16 feet 5	"

Horizontal distance of lifting-shaft, forward of centre line of axle.	4 feet $\frac{3}{4}$	inches.
Centre of lifting-shaft, above centre line of engine..............	$12\frac{1}{2}$	"
Length of hanger...............	14	"
Length of lifting-shaft arms, from centre to centre............	$16\frac{3}{4}$	"
Length of slot in link...........	$18\frac{3}{4}$	"
Width of slot..................	2	"
Horizontal distance from centre of lifting-shaft to centre of rocker	$16\frac{3}{4}$	"
Upper rocker-arm set back.......	$\frac{1}{8}$	"
Cylinder elevated to the foot.....	$\frac{3}{16}$	"
Point of suspension, back toward axle.....................	$\frac{3}{16}$	"
Diameter of main crank-pin journal	$3\frac{3}{4}$	"
Length of main rod $3\frac{1}{2}$ times the length of stroke............	70, 77, 84	"
Length of journal of main crank-pin......................	4	"
Parallel-rod journals, diameter and length....................	3	"
Wrist-pin of cross-head.........	$3\frac{1}{4}$	"
Length	3	"
Driving-axles (diameter)........	$6\frac{1}{2}$	"
Truck-axles (diameter)..........	4	"
Length of boiler................	19 feet 7	"
Length of smoke-arch...........	38	"
Diameter of boiler..............	47	"
Rise of wagon-top above cylinder part of boiler..............	8	"

Steam-dome diameter...........	26 inches.
Height, omitting cap of dome.....	30 "
Length of fire-box, outside.......	68 "
Width of fire-box, outside, being the greatest width admissable between the frames of a 4-foot 8½-inch guage..............	40 "
Water-space, between furnace-sheets.....................	3 "
Length of flues..................	11 feet.
Diameter of flues, inside.........	1¾ "
Number of flues.................	150
Height of crown-sheet, above top of grate-bars...............	57 "
Surface of fire-grate.............	13 11/13 square feet.
Heating surface of fire-box.......	83⅞ " "
Heating surface of flues.........	756 " "
Total heating surface......	839⅞ " "

In this calculation the space of fire-box door, and area of the flue opening in the fire-box in the flue-sheet, are deducted from total area.

This will give 4 17/100 square feet heating surface to 1 inch of cylinder; or 52 49/100 square feet to 1 inch of bore of cylinder.

Total weight of engine, with 3 guages of water in boiler....	65,000 pounds.
Number of gallons of water in boiler.....................	950
Diameter of nozzles.............	2⅞ inches.

Weight on drivers, with water...	41,050 pounds.
Weight on engine truck.........	23,950 pounds.
Height to top of stack from the rail	14 feet 3 inches.
Diameter of body of stack.......	15 "
Diameter of top of stack........	28 "
Diameter of largest part of stack..	48 "
Diameter of petticoat, or lift-pipe.	10½ "
Diameter of flare of bottom of petticoat	19 "
Position of petticoat, from top of boiler	2½ "

Bottom set at the fourth row of flues from the bottom.

——:o:——

IMPORTANT DIMENSIONS OF A LOCOMOTIVE ENGINE,

For cylinders 18 x 24, 19 x 22, 17 x 26, 20 x 20, four-wheel connected engine:

Diameter of cylinder............	18 inches.
Length of stroke................	24 "
Steam ports; length of ports 1 inch less than bore of cylinder....	1¼ x 17 "
Exhaust ports; length of ports 1 inch less than bore of cylinder	2½ x 17 "
Outside lap....................	1 "
Inside lap, line and line, or.......	1/32 "
Throw of eccentric..............	5¼ "

Lead, in full stroke		$\frac{1}{16}$	inches.
Horizontal distance, from centre of axle to centre of rocker	5 feet	$9\frac{1}{4}$	"
Centre of rocker, above center line of engine		$6\frac{1}{4}$	"
Length of rocker-arms		$10\frac{1}{4}$	"
Radius of centre of link	5 feet	5	"
Knuckle-joint centres, back of centre line of link, toward axle		$2\frac{1}{2}$	"
Distance between knuckle-joint centres		$13\frac{1}{2}$	"
Length of eccentric-rods, from centre of eccentric-strap to centre of knuckle-joints	5 feet	$6\frac{3}{4}$	"
Horizontal distance of lifting-shaft, forward of centre line of axle	4 feet	5	"
Centre of lifting-shaft, above centre line of engine		$11\frac{1}{2}$	"
Length of hanger		$15\frac{5}{8}$	"
Length of lifting-shaft arms, from centre to centre		$16\frac{7}{8}$	"
Length of slot in link		19	"
Width of slot		2	"
Horizontal distance from centre of lifting-shaft to centre of rocker		$16\frac{1}{8}$	"
Upper rocker-arm, set back		$\frac{1}{16}$	"
Cylinder elevated to the foot		$\frac{1}{14}$	"
Point of suspension, back toward axle		$\frac{1}{16}$	"
Diameter of main crank-pin journal		$4\frac{1}{4}$	"

Length of main rod 3½ times the length of stroke.		
Length of journal of main crank-pin	4¼	inches.
Parallel-rod journals, diameter and length	3½	"
Wrist-pin of cross-head	3½	"
Length	3½	"
Driving-axles (diameter)	7	"
Truck-axles (diameter)	5	"
Length of boiler	20 feet 7	"
Length of smoke arch	39	"
Diameter of boiler	49½	"
Rise of wagon-top above cylinder part of boiler	8	"
Steam-dome diameter	28	"
Height, omitting cap of dome	30	"
Length of fire-box, outside	72	"
Width of fire-box outside, being the greatest width admissable between the frames of a 4-foot 8½-inch guage	40	"
Water-space between furnace-sheets	3	"
Length of flues	11 feet 4	"
Diameter of flues, inside	1¾	"
Number of flues	174	
Height of crown-sheet above top of grate-bars	59	"
Surface of fire grate	15⅗	square feet.

Heating surface of fire-box.......	$94\frac{5}{10}$	square feet
Heating surface of flues.........	903	" "
Total Heating surface...	$997\frac{5}{10}$	" "

In this calculation the space of fire-box door, and area of the flue opening in the fire-box in the flue-sheet, are deducted from total area.

This will give 4 square feet of heating surface to 1 inch area of cylinder, or 55 $\frac{35}{100}$ square feet to 1 inch of bore of cylinder.

Total weight of engine with 3 guages of water in boiler.....	69,800 pounds.
Number of gallons of water in boiler......	1,200
Diameter of nozzles.............	$3\frac{1}{4}$ inches.
Weight on drivers, with water...	42,500 pounds.
Weight on engine truck.........	27,300 pounds.
Height to top of stack from the rail.......................	14 feet 3 inches.
Diameter of body of stack.......	17 "
Diameter of top of stack........	29 "
Diameter of largest part of stack.	48 "
Diameter of petticoat, or lift-pipe.	$12\frac{1}{2}$ "
Diameter of flare of bottom of petticoat.....................	22 "
Position of petticoat from top of boiler.....................	$2\frac{1}{2}$ "

Bottom set at the fourth row of flues from the bottom.

Exhaust Nozzles.

Exhaust nozzles are a very important part of a Locomotive, and they should be large enough. If too small will choke the engine by the back pressure, which will take considerable of the power of the engine to overcome; besides, it will cause a great waste in fuel.

——:o:——

Clearance of Exhaust.

If the cone in stack be too large, it will not give proper clearance to the exhaust; or if the top of the stack be too small, it will choke the exhaust to such an extent as will take a great portion of the power of the engine to overcome; also will consume double the quantity of fuel.

——:o:——

Boiler.

The boiler is the most important part of a Locomotive Engine, and should be large enough. The proper results of an engine depend, in a great degree, on the boiler being capable of generating a sufficient amount of steam, without contracting the exhaust nozzles to such extent as to choke the engine in the exhaust. When the boiler is not large enough there is a great waste in fuel as well as of power. The Locomotive boiler consists of three parts: the barrel, or cylinder, containing the flues; the fire-box, and smoke-box. The barrel, smoke-box, and outside shell of fire-box, are made of steel or iron, of the best quality, from $\frac{3}{8}$-inch to $\frac{1}{2}$-inch thick, riveted together with $\frac{3}{4}$-inch rivets, placed $1\frac{3}{4}$ inches apart. The inside shell of fire-box is made of the best Sligo iron or steel, from $\frac{5}{16}$-inch to $\frac{7}{16}$-inch thick; or of copper, $\frac{3}{8}$-inch to $\frac{1}{2}$-inch thick. The flue-sheet, when made of copper, for the furnace end, is made of $\frac{1}{2}$-inch or $\frac{5}{8}$-inch thickness. The furnace is made square, the crown-sheet being strengthened by riveting stay-bars to it, with $\frac{7}{8}$-inch rivets, placed 4 inches apart, from centre to centre of rivets. The crown-bars run cross-wise the crown-sheet, and are made of wrought iron, 4 inches deep in the centre, and $3\frac{1}{2}$ inches at the ends, by $\frac{7}{8}$ or 1-inch wide, and are made in pairs, welded together at the ends; they are so cut that the ends will rest on the vertical side sheets of fire-box, and are raised $1\frac{1}{4}$ inches above the crown-sheet, washers being placed between the crown-sheet and bars, at each rivet. The bars are raised, so as to allow the water to circulate as much as possible on the top of the crown-sheet. The outside and inside shell of furnace are separated, for admitting a 3-inch water-space between them, and the two are united by a bar of wrought iron, 3 inches wide by 2 inches deep, riveted between them at the bottom. The inside shell of furnace is also secured to the outside sheet by stay-bolts, $\frac{7}{8}$-inch in diameter, which are screwed through both sheets, and riveted, spaced 4 inches apart from centre to centre. This is termed high-pressure stayed. In stationary and other low-pressure boilers, the stay-bolts are placed from 8 to 11 inches from centre to centre, which is termed low-pressure stayed. The flues occupy about two-thirds of the cylinder part of the boiler; the other third remaining above the flues for water and steam room. The flues are placed in rows, $\frac{5}{8}$-inch being the distance between any two flues; the length of flues varying from 10 to 13 feet, according to the designers' ideas. As a general rule, for engines, with cylinders from 14 to 18 inches in diameter, the 11-foot flue is used; the external diameter being 2 inches. The smoke-box comprises the front end of the cylinder part of boiler, forward of the front flue-sheet, occupying about 38 inches of the length of boiler. The head of front flue-sheet is made of $\frac{1}{2}$-inch iron, flanged around the edge, to rivet to the cylinder part of boiler. The front end of smoke-box has a ring made of 2-inch square wrought iron, riveted on the inside, for the purpose of strengthening the front end, and staying the cylinders, to which the plate holding the door is bolted. For the convenience of cleaning the boiler, four large hand-holes, oval in shape, $3\frac{1}{2}$ x $2\frac{1}{2}$ inches, are cut, one in each bottom corner of leg of boiler, and one in the bottom of front flue-sheet, which are much larger than the screw-plug formerly used. Practice has shown that the former screw-plug, about 2 inches in diameter, was too small to ensure a proper cleaning.

To complete the stay of boiler, I must mention a series of horizontal stay-bolts, from the back boiler-head to the front flue-sheet. They are 8 in number, made of 1-inch round iron; they are attached to the sheets by crow-feet riveted to the sheets, with 2 rivets; an eye on the end of rods, for an inch bolt to go through. There are also 12 stay-rods, six on each side, running on an angle from the crown-bars to top of boiler. The steam-dome is placed over the centre of crown-sheet, stayed with 8 vertical ⅞-inch round iron rods, 4 on each side, running from the crown-bars to the sides of the dome. The dome-cap, or cover, is made of cast iron, held down by ⅞-inch studs, 4½ inches from centre to centre of studs, which are tapped into a solid ring, made of 2-inch square wrought iron, which is riveted to the top inside of dome; the bolts are on the outside of the joint. By this arrangement the steam has no access to them, and they are preserved from corrosion and rust. The same arrangement, for the preserving of bolts holding down the steam-chest cover, by casting sockets on the inside of the steam-chest for the bolts to pass through which come outside of the joints, so as the steam will not have access to them. In consequence of this they can be unscrewed, if necessary, without breaking.

Framing.

The frame of a Locomotive, to which the boiler and machinery are attached, is made of the best hammered wrought iron; and generally made in two pieces, jointed firmly at the forward pedestal, when for an 8-wheel engine, meaning four driving-wheels and a truck with four wheels. When six-wheel, connected with four-wheel truck, or the ten-wheel engine, as it is termed; and the Mogul engine, with six driving-wheels connected, with half-truck with two wheels, are jointed back of the middle pedestal. This is done for the convenience of taking down the back ends, or that part of frame which surrounds the furnace. When rebuilding or repairing the furnace the frames are strong, and firmly braced and bolted to its place. One of the superiorities of an engine consists in the proper proportioning of material, and the strong manner in which all parts are united and secured together. To produce strength, firmness, and steadiness of motion, the length of pedestal being at least 4½ inches longer than the driving-boxes, to prevent the box from striking the top or bottom of frame, when oscillating. The springs used are similar to the ordinary carriage spring, with plates, held together at the centre by a band, and are allowed to slide on each other at the ends; the upper plate terminates with a tip or flange, to prevent the hanger, or spring-strap from slipping off; the lower end of hanger is attached to the under side of the frame by a pin passing through ends of hanger. The centre of the spring rests upon a saddle that astrides the frame, the ends of saddle setting in recesses on the edges of driving-boxes, the other end of spring being attached to the equalizing-beam, which are about twice the length of the driving-spring, to effect an easy-riding engine. A very essential quality in a Locomotive, is to have an equal distribution of the weight upon the wheels. In the Mogul, or ten-wheel engine, the driving-wheels carry four-fifths of the total weight, and the engine-truck one-fifth; one-fifth being sufficient to keep the truck-wheels from climbing the rail. The truck of an eight-wheel engine carries a little over one-third of the total weight, leaving less than two-thirds for the driving-wheels, about one-third for the back drivers, and a little less than one-third for the front drivers. The axles only bear against the top of the driving-box, which are lined with brass, 1½ inches thick, the bottom of box forming a reservoir or cellar, as it is termed, underneath the bearing, filled with oil and waste, to lubricate the journal. The upper part of the box has a reservoir for oil, also, which is supplied to the journal by holes drilled down through the brass. The Locomotive driving wheels vary in size, from 38 inches to 75 inches in diameter; 75 inches being about the largest used in this country; and are invariably made of cast iron, with hollow spokes, using iron or steel tires, from 2½ to 3 inches in thickness. It is necessary to mention that chilled tires are used on some roads, for switch engines. The engine truck-wheels are cast iron, with chilled faces, generally; sometimes steel tires are used on the leading truck-wheels, for an engine running very fast trains, as it is believed, by some master mechanics, that they are safer. There has been much controversy in regard to the question of which has the superiority: the four or six-wheel connected-engine, in regard to moving cars and safeness. It is most probable that the question will remain for some time to come for a decision, as each party claim equal advantages.

The four-wheel connected-engine is preferable for fast running; they also curve easier, and it is claimed that the four-wheel engine will make more trips in the year than the six-wheel connected-engine; consequently, they will move as many cars, at less expense, when including the wear of machinery and of track. There is no doubt that the Locomotives are now becoming too heavy in weight to be supported by four driving-wheels, without doing injury to the machinery and rails. There can be an equal damage done with the six-wheel connected-engine; for, when the rail is greasy, or partially wet, the engineer is required to increase the adhesion by using sand on the rail, and a greater strain is thus produced than can exist in the case of a four-wheel engine, more particularly when on a curve. It is necessary to make the middle or forward tire without a flange, to facilitate the moving of the engine around curves.

Locomotive Tender.

A tender for a Locomotive should be large enough; generally they are too small in the water-space. The coal or wood-space can be less, in most cases. The water-space should be capable of holding 125 gallons for each inch of diameter of cylinder. That will give, for a cylinder 16 inches in diameter: 16 x 125= 2,200 gallons; which will be 200 more gallons than they now hold. The common mode of connecting the engine to the tender, is by means of a draw-bar, with an eye at each end, which enters the draw-head castings of the engine and tender, and held together by a pin passing through the draw-head casting and eye of draw-bar. The buffers of the engine and tender should be closely joined together, as it contributes greatly to prevent oscillation and other irregular motions of the engine.

The best safeguard against excessive oscillation is to have the driving-wheels properly counterbalanced. The weight of tenders varies according to their construction. The weight of tenders for 15, 16, and 17-inch cylinders, without water or fuel, varies from 18, 000 to 22,000 lbs. The tender-trucks should be placed under the tender so as to have nearly an equal weight on each truck, when loaded with fuel and water.

WILLIAM S. HUDSON'S PATENT LOCOMOTIVE,

For Road Construction or Switching Purposes.

:0:

BUILT AT THE ROGERS LOCOMOTIVE WORKS, PATERSON, N. J.

ENGINE "COPIAPO,"

Built at The Rogers Locomotive Works.

Cylinder 15 x 20.
Six driving-wheels, 40 inches in diameter.
Two-wheel truck forward.
Two-wheel truck rear.

Weight of Engine Empty.

Weight on forward truck..............	6,051 lbs.
Weight on front driving-wheels........	15,806 lbs.
Weight on middle driving-wheels.......	17,380 lbs.
Weight on back driving-wheels.........	17,380 lbs.
Weight on rear truck..................	5,040 lbs.
Total weight.................	61,651 lbs.

Weight in running order, with two gauges of water in boiler (about 701 gallons).

Water in tank 1,600 gallons, and 3,800 pounds of coal.

Weight on forward truck..............	9,172 lbs.
Weight on forward drivers.............	21,110 lbs.
Weight on middle drivers.............	23,111 lbs.
Weight on back drivers...............	23,111 lbs.
Weight on back truck................	7,357 lbs.
Total weight of engine........	83,861 lbs.

MOULDING AND CASTING.

Moulding and casting the cylinders of the Locomotive are of more importance than all other castings, and require more ingenuity to make the mould and the cores, and secure them in their places in such manner as to allow the gases to escape as they become heated. The cylinders are cast in dry loam, which is done by building the mould of brick, and facing the brick on the inside with loam. This method of moulding does not require a complete pattern, as the form of the casting can be determined by sweeps and templates. The preparation of the loam is a very important part of the construction; it is composed of coarse, medium, and fine sands, with a mixture of clay, water, and sawdust, with some other ingredidients; the whole is brought to the consistency of mortar; the requirements of the loam are porosity, to allow the gases to escape. After the form of the mould is completed it is placed in an oven and kept under a certain heat until baked, then taken out, and the cores placed in their respective places. The form is now ready to receive the metal. A single mistake, or the slightest carelessness, may cause the loss of the casting.

——:o:——

ECCENTRIC.

There is securely fastened to the driving-shaft, with keys or set-screws, a contrivance called an eccentric, which serves to transfer a reciprocating motion to the slide-valve. Upon close inspection, it appears that this is only a mechanical shift for a crank. The Locomotive has two eccentrics, one for the forward motion, and the other for the backward motion, for each cylinder, fixed firmly upon the driving-shaft. The motion of the eccentric is transferred to the valve direct or indirect; in case of indirect, the motion is transferred by means of the rock-shaft. When direct, the motion is transferred direct to the valve, as the valve-rod is connected to the link by means of a fork-end valve-rod. Direct motion is applied to an inside-connected Locomotive engine. When the steam-chests lie between the cylinders, the valve stands vertical, or in other words, the valve works on the side of the cylinder. In this case, it is necessary to use springs to keep the valves up to their places, when not using steam. The eccentrics and eccentric-straps are made of good cast iron metal. The eccentrics are generally cast solid; the straps are made in two halves, secured together by bolts with jam-nuts; some prefer to have the bolts tapped or screwed through one lug of the strap, and use one jam-nut. There is a dowel-pin fitted in the lugs of the eccentric-straps, to keep them in their proper places. It is well to put three or four pieces of tin between the lugs before they are turned out, for the convenience of adjustment, or taking up the lost motion.

ADMISSION OF STEAM FROM THE BOILER TO THE CYLINDERS.

The admission of steam, from the boiler to the cylinders, is regulated by the common slide, or poppet valve, which is called a throttle-valve, when used for this purpose, which is opened and shut with a hand lever, and is controlled by the engineer, the valve being placed in the dome or in the smoke-box, as desired. The throttle-box, as it is termed, that contains the throttle-valve, is attached to the dry-pipe, which receives the steam from the highest part of the steam-dome, and conveys the steam through two branch-pipes, one for each cylinder, that conveys the steam to the cylinders.

—— :o: ——

HOW STEAM IS ADMITTED INTO CYLINDERS.

Steam is admitted into the cyliuders by means of the plain slide-valve, which is a device by which the receiving and discharging of the steam is regulated, for the opposite ends of the cylinder, and it is called the D valve; it derives its name from the resemblance of a half circle, or D, in the exhaust cavity, which sets over the ports or openings which convey the steam to and from the cylinders, which are three in number. The middle port is termed the exhaust-port; the other two are termed the steam-ports. The effect, then, of moving the valve backwards and forwards, over the ports, as is done by the eccentrics, is to establish a passage alternately between each cylinder-port and the exhaust passage, whereby the steam escapes. And while the steam is escaping from one end of the piston, the position of the valve is such that a free communication exists between the boiler and the other end or side of piston. The piston is, therefore, forced backward and forward in the cylinder, alternately, the valves so changing their position, before the piston arrives at the end of its stroke, that the pressure is by that time thrown to the reverse side of the piston, so as to force it into motion in the opposite direction The valve does not move forward when the piston does, nor does it move forward when the piston moves back, but it moves from the lead line to the extremity of its travel, and back again; while the piston only makes a movement one way, from one end of cylinder to the other.

——:o:——

CLEARANCE.

The term clearance is used to express the extent of the space which exist between the piston, at the extreme end of stroke and the cylinder-head, and the valve-face, or the cubic contents of the steam-passage and the unoccupied portion of the cylinder by the piston. For each stroke of piston this space must be filled with steam, which in no way tends to improve

6

the action of the engine, but rather increases the amount of steam to be exhausted on the return stroke. It becomes necessary to make the valve-face as near to the bore of cylinder as possible, and have as small a space between the piston and cylinder-head, to reduce the cubic contents of the passage to its smallest capacity.

LATERAL MOTION.

Lateral motion is understood to be the clearance or distance between the rails and flanges of driving and truck-wheels. Practice has shown that roads with heavy curves require at least three-quarters of an inch, to enable the engine to run the curves; the back drivers are given one-eighth of an inch less than the forward drivers.

LINK MOTION.

The link motion may be classed as two motions, viz:

First. The stationary link, with shifting block.

Second. The shifting link, with stationary block.

The stationery link, with a shifting block, is a direct motion; the valve-rod taking hold of the link-block by means of a fork end valve-rod. The stationary link motion has a constant lead for all the notches for forward and back motion, which is obtained by curving the link to the radius of the valve-rod, taking the distance from centre of knuckle-joint of valve-rod to centre of link-block, which gives the radius of the link. The position of the eccentric of direct motion is the reverse to that of indirect motion. By drawing a line from the full throw of the eccentric, through the centre of axle of an indirect motion, and then turn the eccentric just half way round, to the position corresponding with the line through centre of axle, will be the position of the eccentric of a direct motion, when using the same lap and lead. In other words, the eccentrics of direct motion are moved from the right angle position of the crank, to get the required lead; while the indirect eccentric is moved to the crank to get the required lead. Should there be no lap or lead in consideration, then, in both cases, the eccentric would be exactly at the right angle position to the crank, or one-fourth of a circle from the crank. The eccentric of direct motion leads the crank; that of indirect follows the crank. The lifting link, with stationary block attached to the lower arm of rock-shaft, which transfers the motion of eccentric to the valve, is the link used on Locomotives generally in the United States. In the shifting link the lead varies with the working of the steam expansively, the greater degree of expansion; that is, the less the admission, the greater, also, is the lead. The lead is least in full-stroke, and greatest in mid-gear;

and the motion can be so adjusted that the same lead is obtained for the back stroke as that of the front stroke, for cutting-off at the various points of stroke; this equality is obtained by locating the centre of saddle-stud, or point of suspension, as it is termed, and by making the radius of the link about three-quarters of an inch to the foot less radius than the horizontal distance between the centre of axle and the centre of lower locker-arm stud, or link-block pin. This reduction is to assist to equalize the cut-off. The motion of the link is composed of a compound motion of the eccentrics, and is governed mostly by the eccentric-rod that is nearest to the link-block. When the block is in the centre of the link the motion is composed equally of the two eccentric-rods, and gives the smallest amount of motion that is given to the valve. The various percentages of admission of steam is obtained by shifting the link on the block, or shifting the block in the link; the nearer the block is to the end of link the greater the motion, or travel of valve, and admission of steam, as the steam varies with the travel of valve. The point of suspension of the link has the greatest influence in regulating an equal distribution of steam. The position of the point of suspension, or locating the centre of stud on the saddle, is fonnd by clamping the saddle to the link temporarily, until the cut-off is set, which locates the point of suspension. The distribution is effected slightly by the length of connecting-rod, in relation to that of the crank. By shortening the connecting-rod and throw of crank, we increase the back stroke admission, and the less is the admission for the front stroke ; therefore, the term link motion, so far as it involves the relation of the valve motion, to that of the connecting-rod and crank, includes the proportion of the crank motion.

Some builders give unequal laps, the front end of valve having more lap than the back end of valve. This is done to equalize the opening and closing of steam-ports. This is not necessary, as it is done by the proper locating of the point of suspension and curvature of link, which has just been described.

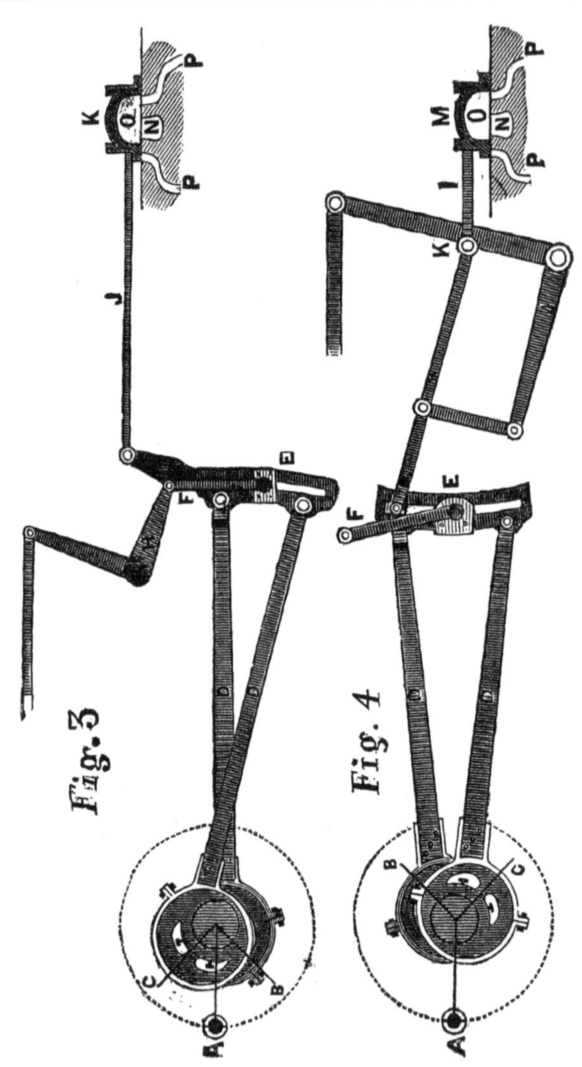

Fig. 3

Fig. 4

Explanation of Figs. 3 and 4.

Fig. 3 is indirect motion, the rock-shaft being used. This link motion is in general use in the United States. *A*, the crank-pin, on the back centre. *B*, the full throw of forward eccentric, which follows the crank. *C*, the full throw of back motion eccentric, which leads the crank when the engine is moving forward. *D*, the eccentric-rods. *E*, the link. *F*, link-hanger. *H*, lifting-shaft. *I*, rocker-shaft. *J*, the valve-rod. *K*, showing the valve on lead-line on back steam-port. *O*, throat of valve. *N*, exhaust port. *P*, steam-ports.

Fig 4 is direct motion, the valve-rod taking hold of link-block by means of a fork-end valve-rod. *A*, the crank-pin, on back centre. *B*, the full throw of forward eccentric, which leads the crank-pin. (It will be observed that the full throw of eccentric is right the reverse of that shown on Fig. 3.) *C*, the full throw of back motion eccentric, which is also reverse to that shown by Fig. 3; still the valve is on the lead-line at the same end of cylinder, the rocker-shaft causing this change of position of eccentrics, as it is plainly seen, when using the rock-shaft; if the full throw of eccentrics be moved forward, to the same position as shown by Fig. 4, then the lower rocker-arm would be forward, and the upper arm of rocker would be moved back, and the lead-line would be given to the front steam-port, instead of the back port; not like the direct motion, when the full throw of eccentrics moves forward the valve moves forward also; consequently, when the rocker is used, the eccentrics must be placed right to the reverse of direct motion to give the opening of steam-port to right end of cylinder. *D*, eccentric-rods. *E*, link. *F*, hanger. *H*, fork-end of valve-rod. *I*, valve-rod. *J*, lifting-shaft. *K*, knuckle-joint centres of valve-rod. *L*, lifter. *M*, valve, showing lead on back steam-port.

SLIP OF THE LINK.

In planning the link motion it is necessary to reduce the slip of the link as much as possible, without interfering with the equalizing of the cut-off, because the greater the slip the greater will be the wear of the link and block, for the block moves on a fixed circle, while the link raises and falls for each stroke of the engine; therefore the link will slide back and forth on its block. The greatest amount of slip is given when working in full stroke; the slip will grow less as the link-block draws near the centre of the link. The slip may be reduced by increasing the length of link, or reducing the lap. The greatest amount of slip is produced by moving the knuckle-joint centres back from the centre line of link toward axle.

——:o:——

RADIUS OF LINK.

The radius of the link varies much, as there are different opinions entertained in regard to this subject. Some curve the link to the horizontal distance between the centre of axle and centre of rocker; others increase this radius; others deduct about three-quarters of an inch to the foot, making the radius less than the horizontal distance between the centre of axle and centre of rocker. The latter will give the best motion. This reduction is made to assist in equalizing the cut-off.

POINT OF SUSPENSION.

The point of suspension, or the locating of the stud on the saddle, is a very essential point, as it regulates the admission of steam, or in other words, it equalizes the motion of the valve, so as to cut off the steam on the forward and return stroke, at the same distance from each end of stroke, at the various points the engine is set to cut-off at. The point of suspension is either located by the workings of the model, or by fastening the saddle to the link with clamps, temporarily, until the valves are set and the cut-off equalized, which locates the position of centre of stud on the saddle, or point of supension, as it is termed; which varies in its location from the centre line of link to one inch back of centre line of link toward axle, which is caused by the locating and imperfection of the working centres. The greatest variation is caused by the greater distance of the eccentric-rods taking hold of the link, from centre line of links horizontally, toward axle. Those centres vary from 2½ inches to 3½ inches, from centre line of link, according to the design of the builder, which causes the stud on saddle to be moved in the same direction. All saddles are located in the centre of length of link.

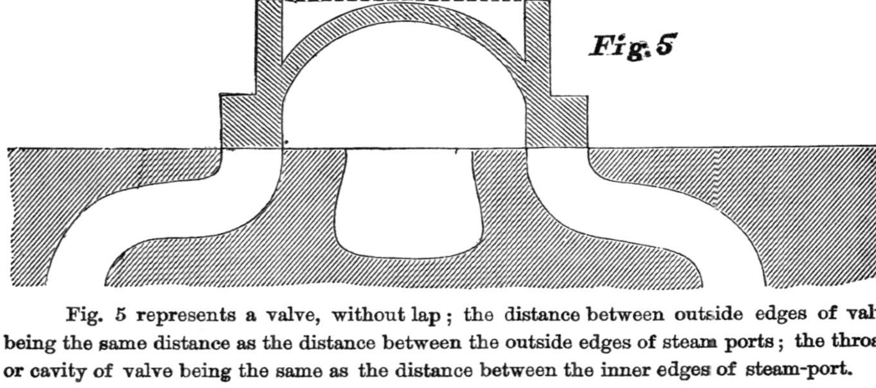

Fig. 5 represents a valve, without lap; the distance between outside edges of valve being the same distance as the distance between the outside edges of steam ports; the throat, or cavity of valve being the same as the distance between the inner edges of steam-port.

LAP.

Lap is an elongation of the valve-face, to a certain extent, over the steam-ports, whereby the port is closed sooner than it would be otherwise. The lap varies from ½ to 1 inch on each end of valve, as the circumstances may require for the motion designed. Lap is chiefly to work the steam expansively. Without lap, when using the single slide or D valve there can be no expansion, because it operates in such a manner that the steam is admitted to the cylinder throughout the whole of each stroke, while the other end is open for the exhaust, and that the exhaust and admission of steam takes place at the same time, at the end of each stroke. In cutting-off at half-stroke, then the valve would be cutting-off the steam at half-stroke from one end of cylinder; at the same time the valve would be just opening to admit steam to the other end of cylinder; and expansion and compression would also take place; at the same time the position of the eccentric would be at a right angle to the crank. By moving the eccentric a little toward the crank, and fastening it there, then the steam would be admitted before the piston reached the end of the stroke. Lap causes the valve to reach the end of its travel, or its full opening of port, for steam and exhaust, earlier in the course of the stroke. For each stroke of the piston there are four distinct events that take place, caused by the moving of the valve over the steam-port: the admission, expansion, compression, and the exhaustion of the steam. The outer edges of the valve and steam-ports work together, and regulate the admission and expansion of the steam; while the inner edges of the valve and of the steam-ports together, determine the points of compression, and release, or opening of exhaust. There is also sometimes, lap given to the inside of the valves, which is termed inside lap; which hastens compression and prolongs expansion. Inside lap never exceeds twenty-five per-cent. of the outside lap; generally there is none, (which is termed line-in-line;) often as much as $\frac{1}{8}$th of an inch less than none, which causes early release, or commencement of exhaust, and exhaust closes, and compression takes place at a later period of the stroke.

——:o:——

LEAD.

This term is applied to the amount of opening the valve has for the admission of steam, when the piston is just beginning its stroke. It is found expedient that the valve should have opened a little to admit steam on the reverse side of the piston, before the stroke terminates, to cause a sufficient amount of compression, to neutralize an effect due to the imperfect workmanship, as well as the continual wear in the boxes of the crank and cross-head wrist pins. The amount of this opening, which is given by turning the eccentric more or less around upon the shaft, is what is termed lead. Lead is a very essential point, and too much should not be given, as it will cause premature or too early admission of steam, which is a great detriment to the working of the engine, as it causes too great amount of counter pressure. The lead requisite may vary for different engines, and also for the same engine, when hauling freight or passenger trains. Lead should not exceed $\frac{1}{8}$-inch, in full stroke, for the link motion, if the engine be required to work in the notches approaching mid-gear.

——:o:——

INCREASE OF LEAD.

Increase of lead is produced by changing the engine from full stroke to mid-gear. The lead will increase from $\frac{1}{16}$th to $\frac{5}{16}$ths of an inch. The length of eccentric rods control the amount of increase of lead. The shorter the eccentric rods the greater will be the increase; it is also impossible, with this motion, to stop the engine, by placing the engine in mid-gear, as one or both valves will give opening of steam-port, to the amount of lead given in full stroke to one port, and the amount of increase of lead added to the same.

The cause of the increase of the lead is that the eccentric rods sweep from different centres; the curves described are different from that which would be sweeping from the centre of the axle, when the engine is on the forward dead-centre, and in mid-gear, the link-block will be in the centre of link, and both eccentric-rods will reach their greatest horizontal distance forward, toward the rocker, while the engine is on the dead-centre; and by raising or lowering the link, the eccentric-straps change their position on the eccentrics, moving the rods from the extreme throw forward, back toward axle, thereby lessening the horizontal reach of the eccentric-rods, from the rocker. Therefore, by changing the motion of engine from full stroke to mid-gear, the lower rocker-arm will move forward, and the upper rocker-arm will move back, which gives the increase of lead. When the engine is on the back dead-centre, and in mid-gear, the link block in centre of link, both eccentric-rods will reach their lesser horizontal distance from the rocker, as the full throw of the eccentrics are in the opposite direction from the rocker, *vice versa* from that when on the forward centre; and by raising or lowering the link to full stroke, the eccentric-straps change their position on the eccentrics, the same as when on the forward centre. Moving the eccentric-rods from their full throw, which causes the eccentric-rods to move ahead toward the rocker the same amount as they move back, when on the forward centre. Therefore, by changing the engine from full stroke to mid-gear, the lower rocker-arm moves back, and the upper rocker-arm moves ahead, giving the same increase of lead to the back port, as given when on the forward centre, to the forward port.

If the rods be changed, so as the back motion rods take hold at the top of the link, instead of the bottom, then the lead will be most in full stroke, instead of mid-gear, *vice versa*, as the movement becomes reversed.

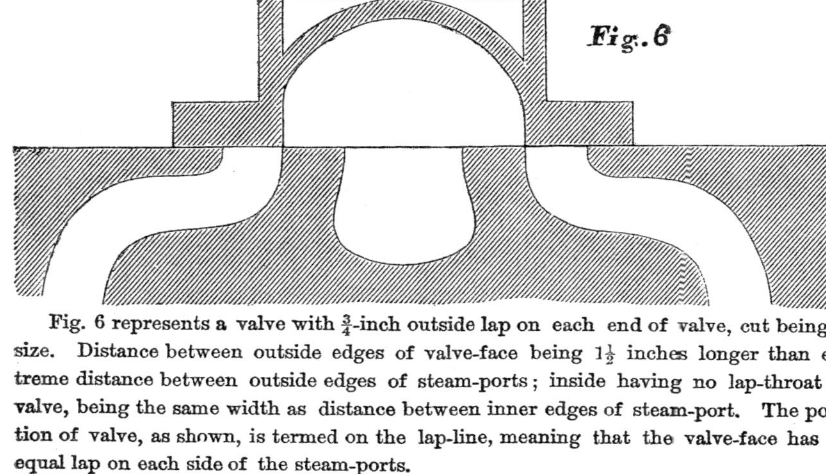

Fig. 6 represents a valve with $\frac{3}{4}$-inch outside lap on each end of valve, cut being $\frac{1}{4}$ size. Distance between outside edges of valve-face being $1\frac{1}{2}$ inches longer than extreme distance between outside edges of steam-ports; inside having no lap-throat of valve, being the same width as distance between inner edges of steam-port. The position of valve, as shown, is termed on the lap-line, meaning that the valve-face has an equal lap on each side of the steam-ports.

COMPRESSION.

Compression is the term used to express the distance the piston moves in the cylinder, after release or exhaust has taken place and the exhaust passage closed by the return stroke of the valve; whereby the communication is cut off from the exhaust-port and that end of cylinder, and compression takes place between the piston and cylinder-head, for a period, at the latter end of stroke. The distance that compression takes place, from end of stroke, is governed by the lap of valve, and the distance that the steam is cut-off from the beginning of the stroke. When working in the full-stroke notch the compression is small, not exceeding 1½ inches of the stroke. Compression increases as the period of expansion is increased, when working in the eighth notch, or cutting off the steam at one-third of the stroke. Compression commences about one-third from end of stroke; therefore the piston works about one-third of the stroke against compression.

—:o:—

COUNTER PRESSURE.

Counter pressure is the resistance given to the piston, which is caused by the admission of steam to the opposite end of cylinder, before the preceding stroke has been finished, caused by having too much lead.

PREMATURE LEAD.

Premature lead is the opening of steam-port to admit steam too early in the course of the preceding stroke. If, from any cause, the valve should open to admit steam to the opposite end of cylinder, prior to the piston reaching the end of its preceding stroke; it is termed premature, or too early lead, and causes a heavy counter pressure, or resistance to the progress of the piston.

——:o:——

LEAD ON EXHAUST.

Lead on exhaust is the opening given to the steam-port by the inner edge of valve-face passing over the inner edge of steam-port, for the pent-up steam to escape, which rushes into the exhaust chamber or cavity of valve, into the exhaust passage, and escapes into the chimney or stack. The amount of opening given, when the engine is on the dead-centre, is termed that amount of lead on exhaust.

——:o:——

CONSTRUCTION OF THE LOCOMOTIVE.

First. The boiler is placed on the construction track, and leveled by the barrel, or cylinder part, and plumbed by the sides of the furnace.

Second. The frames are placed in their position, and leveled by the top side, and squared by the centre of pedestal jaws; lines being drawn the entire length of frame, set by the face of pedestals, to test the correctness of frame, and see if they are parallel, being the same width at both ends, guages being used to keep the frame to its place. The frame is now properly secured to its place by temporary braces and clamps, until the expansion braces have been fitted, and the front ends properly secured to buffer beam. Lines are now drawn, for the purpose of setting up the cylinders, which are drawn from the back end of frame to the buffer beam, set by the face of pedestals, to locate the line centres, so as to set the cylinder line from buffer beam to line board, which is placed in the centre of main driving pedestals. All line centres, for heights, widths, and horizontal distances, for all parts of the engine, are received from the drawing room. When the saddle is independent of the cylinders, it is set by the same line the cylinders are set by, using the same care as when setting the cylinders, it being leveled by the exhaust-pipe faces; cylinders being leveled by the valve-seat faces.

The slides are set up by the cylinder line, and adjusted by means of a long temporary piston-rod, which just fits the piston gland of cylinder-head. The front end of this temporary rod is held to centre of cylinder by means of a spider set in front end of cylinder, being bored out to a proper fit to receive the rod. The back end of rod having been fitted to the cross-head, the slides are how adjusted, so that the cross-head will move back and forth, attached to the rod, without binding.

Third. Fitting up the pumps, rockers, and lifting-shaft, working from cylinder line and centre of pedestal. In the meantime the flues, steam, or dry pipe, and branch pipe, that conveys the steam to cylinders, have all been fitted to their places; the safety-valve is attached to the dome-cap, and the cap is screwed down to its place; gauge-cocks having been tapped and screwed to their places, the first one being located 2½ inches to 3 inches above the highest point of crown-sheet; the second gauge is located 1¾ inches es above the first one; the third gauge 1¾ inches above the second one. The front end of crown-sheet being generally elevated above the back end, varying from one-half inch to two and one-half inches.

Fourth. The boiler is steamed up, to test the workmanship, and caulk such leaks as it may need. The driving-wheels are now placed under the engine; also the engine truck and the engine truck centre, which is bolted to the bottom side of saddle, and is located in the centre of saddle, between the frames. The bottom braces of pedestals being bolted to their places, and wedges properly adjusted, which is done by squaring the wheels, by drawing a line parallel with the pedestal faces and adjusting the main driving-wheels with the wedges, so that the face of tire or driving-wheel, whichever has been faced, is parallel with the line drawn. The other driving-wheels are squared with trams, by placing the centres of axles on both sides, the same distance apart.

The engine is now raised up, so that the wheels are

free from the rail; the driving boxes being properly wedged in the centre of pedestals, so that props can be placed under the bottom of frame, to keep the engine off the track, for the purpose of setting the valves and trying the engine with steam, etc.; side braces being used to keep the engine firm in its place.

Fifth. To get the length of the main rods.

RULE—Place the cross-head in the middle of its travel, which is done by attaching the cross-head to the piston-rod, and moving the cross-head until the piston strikes both cylinder-heads, so as to get the clearance and the middle of its travel. Then take the distance from centre of wrist-pin of cross-head to centre of axle, which will be the length of the main rod.

Length of parallel rods: the distance between the centre of driving axles will be the length of parallel rods.

The length of lifting-shaft arms are not less than the distance the link-block works in the link, or the length of slot in link, deducting the length of link-block.

Length of rocker-arms vary from one and a half times to twice the throw of eccentric, according to the designers' ideas.

LENGTH OF VALVE ROD.

Place the valve on the valve-seat, so as the valve will have an equal lap on both sides of the steam-ports alike, which is termed the lap-line; then place the upper rocker-arm in a right angle position to the alides; take the distance between the centre of rocker-srm pin and the valve, which will be the length of valve rod.

LENGTH OF ECCENTRIC RODS.

Place the upper rocker-arm in a right angle position to the slides; take the distance between the centre of axle, and centre of lower rocker-arm or link-block pin; this will give the length from centre of eccentric-strap to the centre of knuckle-joint of link. By deducting the distance from the centre-line of link to the centre of knuckle-joint of link, will be the proper length of eccentric-rods.

The length may also be taken, by placing the valve on the lap line, so as the valve covers both steam-ports alike; then place the crank-pin on the forward or back dead-centre, and place the extreme throw of eccentrics to the right angle position to the crank, the forward eccentric following the crank; the back eccentric leading the crank-pin; the link is required now to be raised so as the link-block is in the centre of the link, and the knuckle-joint centres both on the same plumb line of engine; take the distance from the centre of knuckle-joint pins to the eccentric-straps, where the eccentric-rods take hold; this gives the length of the eccentric-rods.

——:o:——

LENGTH OF REACH-ROD.

Place the reverse lever in a vertical position; raise the link by the lifting-shaft until the link-block is in the centre of the link; take the distance between the centres of lifting-shaft arm pin and the reverse lever pin, where the reach-rod takes hold; this gives the length of reach-rod.

——:o:——

VALVE SETTING.

Place the crank in a position corresponding to the end of the stroke; or, in other words, place the crank-pin so that it is in a line with the centre of axle and centre of cross-head wrist-pin; this is termed the dead-centre. The most practical way to get the dead-centre is to move the engine ahead, until the cross-head is up to within a quarter of an inch of the full stroke of engine; then scribe a line across the cross-head and slides, and fasten a straight-edge or rule to the top of wheel cover, or any convenient place, so as to scribe a line on the face of the tire; then again move the engine forward over the centre, past the line scribed on the slides; then move the engine back, until the line scribed on the cross-head is to the line that is scribed on the slides; now scribe another line from the same side of rule or straight-edge, on the tire; find the centre between the two lines scribed on the tire; bring this centre to the rule; the engine is now on the dead-centre, or in the position corresponding to the end of stroke. Move the engine again, until the cross-head has reached the other end of the slides; proceed in the same manner as before, scribing from the same side of rule, on the tire. To find that centre, continue in the same manner on the opposite side, by fastening a rule or straight-edge to some convenient place, or on the wheel cover, scribing from the same side of rule each time, to get centres for that engine, scribing on the cross-heads and slides, the same as done for opposite side. We will now proceed to set the valves, by placing the engine on the dead-centre. Next in order, drop the links, so as the link-block will be ½-inch from the end of link, which will allow for the wear of the joints, as the weight is all downward; the crank is thus placed on the dead-centre. The valves must be adjusted so as to have the proper amount of lead, which is required at the commencement of each stroke; the eccentrics must be turned around upon the shaft to their proper place. The best method is to place the full throw of eccentrics to a right angle position to the crank. When commencing to shift the eccentrics for lead, then move the eccentrics forward toward the crank-pin, until the proper lead is obtained; then lengthen or shorten the eccentric-rods, until the same lead, or opening of port is obtained on the back centre that there is when the crank-pin is on the forward centre; it may be possible that two or three shifts may be required to get them just right. In setting the forward motion, the wheels must be moved forward, when coming to the dead centre. In setting the back motion, the wheels must be moved back, when coming to the dead centre, so as to take up all the lost motion. In setting the cut-off, or marking off the circle for the reversal lever latch, which is done after the valves have been set right in full stroke, having an equal lead when the crank is either on the back or forward centre; then proceed to set the valve to cut off the steam at any point of the stroke desired, by moving the engine forward, until the cross-head has reached the point of stroke that the steam is to be cut off at Suppose the engine be required to cut off at 10 inches, move the engine forward until the cross-head has moved 10 inches from end of stroke; lift the link, by the reverse lever, until the valve has just closed the steam opening of the steam-port; then scribe a line on the circle from both sides of the reverse lever latch. Supposing the next point desired to cut off at will be 12 inches: move the engine forward until the cross-head has moved 12 inches from end of stroke; lift the link with the reverse lever again, until the valve has just closed the steam opening of the steam-port, mark the circle again for the notch for the reverse lever latch,

Continue in the same manner until all the desired points have been obtained.

In setting the cut-off it is necessary to move the engine forward, until the cross-head has traveled the full length of stroke, and back again on the return stroke, so as to see if the valve cuts off at the same point of stroke moving forward, that it does in moving back, on the return stroke. Should there be a deviation in cutting off, it can be obviated by shifting the saddle a trifle, from centre line of link toward axle. Then, again, should the saddle have been permanently fixed to the link, so as it cannot be moved, it will be necessary to cut off, accurately, at half stroke, or at the point where the engine is mostly used; this can be done by lengthening or shortening the eccentric-rod, as it may be required.

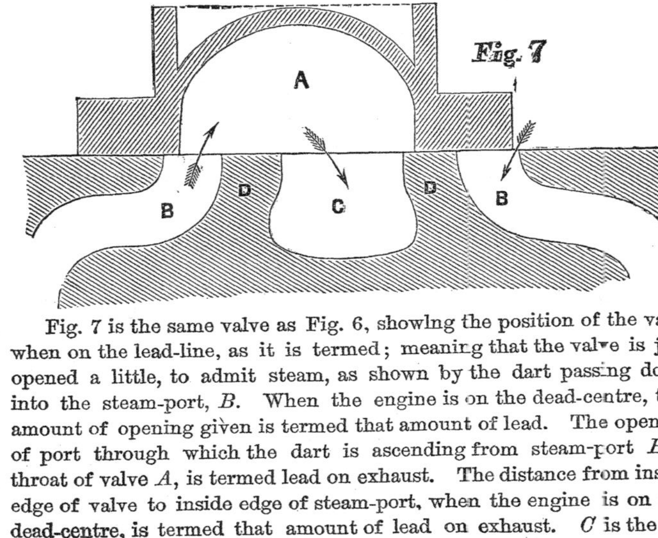

Fig. 7 is the same valve as Fig. 6, showing the position of the valve when on the lead-line, as it is termed; meaning that the valve is just opened a little, to admit steam, as shown by the dart passing down into the steam-port, *B*. When the engine is on the dead-centre, this amount of opening given is termed that amount of lead. The opening of port through which the dart is ascending from steam-port *B* to throat of valve *A*, is termed lead on exhaust. The distance from inside edge of valve to inside edge of steam-port, when the engine is on the dead-centre, is termed that amount of lead on exhaust. *C* is the exhaust port that leads into the exhaust passage to the stack; *D* the bridges, or metal, between steam and exhaust-port.

POSITIONS OF ECCENTRICIS.

To locate the eccentrics to their proper places on the axle, before the wheels are placed under the engine:

Place the centre of crank-pin and centre of axle in a perpendicular line with a plumb-line or level; then place the full throw of eccentrics at the right angle position to the crank-pin, so that the full throw of eccentrics will be in the opposite direction to each other; then drop a plumb-line over the face of each eccentric, if the rocker-shaft be used. Move each eccentric toward the crank, until the distance between the faces of eccentrics and plumb-line measures the distance equal to the lap and lead of one end of the valve, which will be the proper position of eccentrics.

EXAMPLE.—If the eccentrics be 14 inches in diameter, and the throw of eccentrics be 5 inches, then the distance from centre of axle to face of full throw of each eccentric will be $9\frac{1}{2}$ inches, and the horizontal distance from face to face of full throw of eccentrics will be twice $9\frac{1}{2}$ inches, making 19 inches distance between the extreme faces. If we now drop a plumb-line from the face of each eccentric, the lines will be 19 inches apart, the distance the same as eccentric faces. If the lap be $\frac{7}{8}$-inch, and lead $\frac{1}{8}$-inch, on each end of valve, then the lap and lead will be 1 inch; the distance that the eccentrics to be moved from plumb-line toward crank-pin; or, in other words, the extreme distance between faces of eccentrics now, will be 17 inches, instead of 19 inches, each eccentric will measure 8½ inches from centre of axle to a perpendicular line now drawn from faces of eccentrics; or, if the lap be ¾-inch and lead $\frac{1}{16}$-inch, making $\frac{13}{16}$-inch, the distance from faces of eccentrics to plumb-line, or the extreme horizontal distance between faces of eccentrics now will be 17⅜ inches, instead of 19 inches; and the distance from centre of axle to perpendicular line, at face of eccentrics, will be 8$\frac{11}{16}$ inches. If the lap and lead be increased to equal half the throw of eccentric, which will be 2½ inches, 2½ inches then would be the distance required of eccentric to be moved from the perpendicular line drawn at the faces of full throw of eccentrics. This would bring the full throw of eccentrics exactly to the position of the crank, both eccentrics would be in the same position; it is plainly seen that lap and lead causes the full throw of eccentrics to be moved toward each other. It is to be remembered, if the motion be direct, the eccentrics will require to be moved, in the opposite direction, the same distance from the right angle position from the crank.

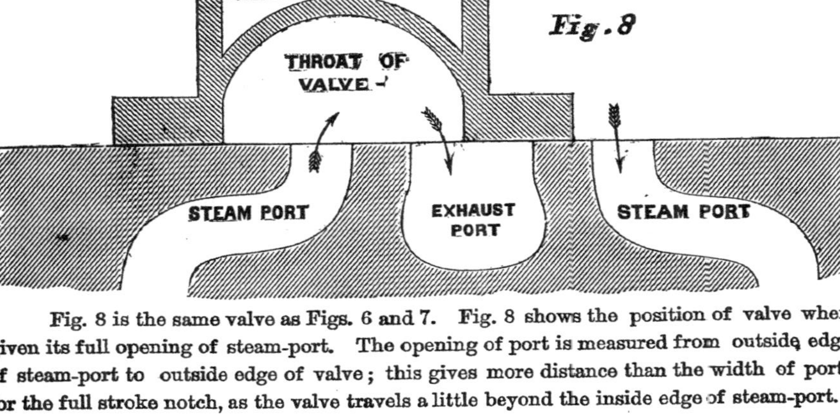

Fig. 8

Fig. 8 is the same valve as Figs. 6 and 7. Fig. 8 shows the position of valve when given its full opening of steam-port. The opening of port is measured from outside edge 8
of steam-port to outside edge of valve; this gives more distance than the width of port, for the full stroke notch, as the valve travels a little beyond the inside edge of steam-port.

TABLES OF LINK MOTION.

Valve tables of link motion, showing the different effects produred in the distribution of steam, with different laps, leads, travel of valves, and points of suspension, or locating the centre of stud on saddle.

Table No. 1, page 115, of link motion, was taken from an engine cylinder 15 inches in diameter; stroke 24 inches; valve having no lap; face of valve being the total length between the extreme outside edges of steam-ports; the width of exhaust cavity, or throat of valve being just the width of extreme distance of inner edges of steam-ports; throw of eccentric 4 inches; lead given, in full stroke, ⅛-inch; rocker-shaft is used; position of eccentrics being nearly at the right angle to the crank-pin. If there was no lead in consideration, then the full throw of eccentric would be just at right angles to the crank-pin, or one-quarter of the circle from the crank-pin; therefore, with this valve, as the table shows, the valve is in the middle of its stroke when the piston is at the end of its stroke, and the valve closes both the steam and exhaust passages, and is ready, with the slightest possible advance, to open, both for the return stroke of the piston. In referring to the table, we find, when cutting-off at any point of the stroke, that the steam will be admitted to the opposite side of piston at the same time; and, when cutting-off at half stroke, the link block will be in the centre of link, and the valve will be in the middle of its stroke, cutting off the steam from one end of

VALVE TABLE OF LINK MOTION—NO. I.

Notches.	Per cent. of admission.	Travel of valve.	Opening of Steam Port		Steam Cuts off. Expansion begins,		Exhaust Opens.		Exhaust closes, and Compression begins		Lead on Steam Port		Lead on Exhaust.		Slip of Link.	Lead commences from end of stroke
			Front Stroke	Back Stroke	Front Stroke	Back Stroke	Front Stroke	Back Stroke	Front Stroke	Back Stroke	Front Stroke	Back Stroke	Front Stroke	Back Stroke		
		Inch.	Inch.	Inch.	Inch.	Inch.	Inch.	Inch.	Inch.	Inch.	Inch.	Inch.	Inch.	Inch.	Inch.	Inch.
1	100	4	$2\frac{1}{16}$	2	24	24	24	24	24	24	$\frac{1}{8}$	$\frac{1}{8}$	$\frac{1}{8}$	$\frac{1}{8}$	$\frac{7}{8}$	0
2	79	$\frac{13}{16}$	$\frac{1}{2}$	$\frac{7}{16}$	19	19	19	19	19	19	$\frac{5}{16}$	$\frac{5}{16}$	$\frac{5}{16}$	$\frac{5}{16}$	$\frac{11}{32}$	5
3	71	$\frac{3}{4}$	$\frac{3}{8}$	$\frac{3}{8}$	17	17	17	17	17	17	$\frac{1}{4}$	$\frac{1}{4}$	$\frac{1}{4}$	$\frac{1}{4}$	$\frac{1}{4}$	7
4	62	$\frac{11}{16}$	$\frac{5}{16}$	$\frac{5}{16}$	15	$15\frac{1}{4}$	15	$15\frac{1}{4}$	15	$15\frac{1}{4}$	$\frac{9}{32}$	$\frac{9}{32}$	$\frac{9}{32}$	$\frac{9}{32}$	$\frac{3}{32}$	9
5	50	$\frac{5}{8}$	$\frac{9}{32}$	$\frac{9}{32}$	12	12	12	12	12	12	$\frac{5}{16}$	$\frac{5}{16}$	$\frac{5}{16}$	$\frac{5}{16}$	$\frac{3}{32}$	12

Table of Link Motion, taken from an Engine cylinder, 15 inches diameter; stroke 24 inches; steam-ports 14x1$\frac{1}{8}$ inches; exhaust ports 14x2$\frac{1}{4}$ inches; throw of eccentric 4 inches; lead $\frac{1}{8}$ inch, in full stroke; stud on saddle 5-32 back of centre line of link, towards axle; valve having no outside or inside lap, the length of valve face being the total length between the extreme outside edges of steam ports; the width of exhaust cavity, or throat of valve, being just the width of distance between the inner edges of steam port; rocker-shaft being used.

the cylinder. when the valve will be just opening to receive steam in the other end of cylinder. The table shows that, when the steam is cut off at half stroke, or any other point of stroke, the exhaust opens at the same time, for the same end of cylinder, and the exhaust closes, and steam is admitted in the opposite end of cylinder all at the same time ; therefore, without laps, we have admission, expansion, release, or exhausting, and compression, all taking place at the same time ; therefore, it becomes necessary to make the valve longer, so as to lap over the steam-ports at both ends, when in the middle of the stroke. By increasing the lead, it would give an earlier release, or, in other words, the exhaust will take place sooner ; this will bring another difficulty, in the shape of premature or too early lead, for the same distance from end of stroke ; that release or exhaust takes place on one end of cylinder, lead would take place the same distance from the other end of cylinder. It is plainly seen that a valve without lap cannot be used for the Locomotive, when using the single valve, as the exhaust or release does not take place at the right time, as it takes place at the end of stroke, and there is no time for the exhaust to take place prior to the end of stroke, and the steam cannot be worked expansively, without lap, for the expansion of steam in the cylinders takes place during the intervals between the suppression and release of the steam admitted to the cylinder. Lap of valve provides expansive action of the steam ; for this object lap is given without lap, when using

VALVE TABLE OF LINK MOTION.—NO. II.

Notches.	Per cent. of admission.	Travel of valve.	Opening of Steam Port		Steam cuts off. Expansion begins.		Exhaust Opens.		Exhaust closes, and compression begins.		Lead on Steam Port		Lead on Exhaust.		Slip of link.	Lead commences from end of stroke
			Front Stroke	Back Stroke	Front Stroke	Back Stroke	Front Stroke	Back Stroke	Front Stroke	Back Stroke	Front Stroke	Back Stroke	Front Stroke	Back Stroke		
		Inch.	Inch.	Inch.	Inch.	Inch.	Inch.	Inch.	Inch.	Inch.	Inch.	Inch.	Inch.	Inch.	Inch.	Inch.
1	95	4	$1\frac{11}{16}$	$1\frac{5}{8}$	$22\frac{7}{8}$	23	$23\frac{5}{8}$	$23\frac{3}{4}$	$23\frac{5}{8}$	$23\frac{3}{4}$	$\frac{1}{16}$	$\frac{1}{16}$	$\frac{7}{16}$	$\frac{7}{16}$	$\frac{5}{8}$	0
2	79	$2\frac{1}{4}$	$\frac{3}{4}$	$\frac{11}{16}$	19	$19\frac{1}{8}$	22	22	22	22	$\frac{3}{16}$	$\frac{3}{16}$	$\frac{9}{16}$	$\frac{9}{16}$	$\frac{1}{4}$	$\frac{1}{4}$
3	71	$1\frac{7}{8}$	$\frac{9}{16}$	$\frac{9}{16}$	17	17	$20\frac{7}{8}$	$20\frac{7}{8}$	$20\frac{7}{8}$	$20\frac{7}{8}$	$\frac{1}{4}$	$\frac{1}{4}$	$\frac{5}{8}$	$\frac{5}{8}$	$\frac{7}{32}$	$\frac{1}{2}$
4	62	$1\frac{11}{16}$	$\frac{1}{2}$	$\frac{1}{2}$	15	15	$19\frac{7}{8}$	$19\frac{7}{8}$	$19\frac{7}{8}$	$19\frac{7}{8}$	$\frac{1}{4}$	$\frac{1}{4}$	$\frac{5}{8}$	$\frac{5}{8}$	$\frac{5}{32}$	$\frac{3}{4}$
5	59	$1\frac{5}{8}$	$\frac{7}{16}$	$\frac{7}{16}$	$13\frac{1}{2}$	$13\frac{1}{2}$	19	19	19	19	$\frac{1}{4}$	$\frac{1}{4}$	$\frac{5}{8}$	$\frac{5}{8}$	$\frac{9}{64}$	$1\frac{1}{8}$
6	50	$1\frac{1}{2}$	$\frac{3}{8}$	$\frac{3}{8}$	12	12	$18\frac{1}{8}$	$18\frac{1}{8}$	$18\frac{1}{8}$	$18\frac{1}{8}$	$\frac{1}{4}$	$\frac{1}{4}$	$\frac{5}{8}$	$\frac{5}{8}$	$\frac{1}{8}$	$1\frac{1}{2}$
7	41	$1\frac{7}{16}$	$\frac{11}{32}$	$\frac{11}{32}$	10	10	17	$16\frac{7}{8}$	17	$16\frac{7}{8}$	$\frac{1}{4}$	$\frac{1}{4}$	$\frac{5}{8}$	$\frac{5}{8}$	$\frac{7}{64}$	2
8	33	$1\frac{3}{8}$	$\frac{5}{16}$	$\frac{5}{16}$	8	8	15	$15\frac{1}{16}$	15	$15\frac{1}{16}$	$\frac{1}{4}$	$\frac{1}{4}$	$\frac{5}{8}$	$\frac{5}{8}$	$\frac{3}{32}$	3

Cylinder 15 inches diameter; stroke 24 inches; steam-ports 14x1⅛ inches; exhaust-ports 14x2¼ inches; throw of eccentric 4 inches; lead 1-16 inch, in full stroke; stud on saddle ⅛ inch back of centre line of link, towards axle; outside lap ⅝ inch on each end of valve, face being ¾ inch longer than the extreme distance between the outside edges of steam-port, inside having no lap; width of cavity, or throat of valve, the total distance between the inner edges of steam-ports, rocker-shaft being used.

the common D, or slide valve, there can be no expansion, as the table shows, because then the compression and the release of steam admitted to one end of cylinder, occurs at the same time. There is no difficulty in getting steam into the cylinders, as the steam rushes in, corresponding with the travel of piston. After the steam has exerted its force, it is then required to have a free and rapid departure, by having a wide passage before the piston has reached the end of its stroke.

TABLE No. 2.—In referring to this table we find what may be called a short lap valve, as the lap is much shorter than is used in a Locomotive with link motion, it being a $\frac{3}{8}$th lap valve, having $\frac{3}{8}$-inch on each end, the length of valve-face being $\frac{3}{4}$ of an inch longer than the extreme distance between the outside edges of steam-ports, the inside having no lap, the throat or cavity of valve being the same width as the distance between the inner edges of steam-ports; lead $\frac{1}{16}$-inch in full stroke, rock shaft being used; diameter of cylinder 15 inches; stroke 24 inches; throw of eccentric 4 inches, being the same motion as Table No. 1, except the increase of lap. In referring to tables, we find a very different motion, as Table No. 2 shows that we have gained the position required for the valve for admission of steam, for all the notches, nearly to half stroke; we also find a decided improvement toward working the steam expansively, as the table shows, from the fourth to the eighth notch. That twenty-five per cent. of the distance that the steam follows the

VALVE TABLE OF LINK MOTION—NO. III.

Notches.	Per cent. of admission.	Travel of valve.	Opening of Steam Port		Steam cuts off, Expansion begins.		Exhaust Opens.		Exhaust closes, and compression begins.		Lead on Steam Port		Lead on Exhaust.		Slip of Link	Lead commences from end of stroke
			Front Stroke	Back Stroke	Front Stroke	Back Stroke	Front Stroke	Back Stroke	Front Stroke	Back Stroke	Front Stroke	Back Stroke	Front Stroke	Back Stroke		
		Inch.	Inch.	Inch.	Inch.	Inch.	Inch.	Inch.	Inch.	Inch.	Inch.	Inch.	Inch.	Inch.	Inch.	Inch.
1	91	4	$1\frac{3}{4}$	$1\frac{5}{8}$	$21\frac{7}{8}$	22	$22\frac{7}{8}$	23	$22\frac{7}{8}$	23	$\frac{3}{8}$	$\frac{3}{8}$	$\frac{3}{4}$	$\frac{3}{4}$	$\frac{5}{8}$	$\frac{1}{8}$
2	79	$2\frac{7}{8}$	$1\frac{1}{16}$	1	19	$19\frac{1}{8}$	$21\frac{1}{2}$	$21\frac{1}{2}$	$21\frac{1}{2}$	$21\frac{1}{2}$	$\frac{1}{2}$	$\frac{1}{2}$	$\frac{7}{8}$	$\frac{7}{8}$	$\frac{3}{8}$	$\frac{3}{4}$
3	71	$2\frac{1}{2}$	$\frac{7}{8}$	$\frac{27}{32}$	17	$17\frac{1}{16}$	$20\frac{1}{4}$	$20\frac{1}{4}$	$20\frac{1}{4}$	$20\frac{1}{4}$	$\frac{17}{32}$	$\frac{17}{32}$	$\frac{29}{32}$	$\frac{29}{32}$	$\frac{1}{4}$	$1\frac{1}{2}$
4	62	$2\frac{1}{4}$	$\frac{23}{32}$	$\frac{23}{32}$	15	15	19	19	19	19	$\frac{9}{16}$	$\frac{9}{16}$	$\frac{15}{16}$	$\frac{15}{16}$	$\frac{3}{16}$	$2\frac{1}{8}$
5	59	$2\frac{1}{8}$	$\frac{11}{16}$	$\frac{11}{16}$	$13\frac{1}{2}$	$13\frac{1}{2}$	$17\frac{3}{4}$	$17\frac{3}{4}$	$17\frac{3}{4}$	$17\frac{3}{4}$	$\frac{9}{16}$	$\frac{9}{16}$	$\frac{15}{16}$	$\frac{15}{16}$	$\frac{5}{32}$	$2\frac{7}{8}$
6	50	2	$\frac{5}{8}$	$\frac{5}{8}$	12	12	$16\frac{3}{4}$	$16\frac{3}{4}$	$16\frac{3}{4}$	$16\frac{3}{4}$	$\frac{9}{16}$	$\frac{9}{16}$	$\frac{15}{16}$	$\frac{15}{16}$	$\frac{7}{8}$	$3\frac{1}{2}$
7	41	$1\frac{15}{16}$	$\frac{19}{32}$	$\frac{19}{32}$	10	10	15	15	15	15	$\frac{9}{16}$	$\frac{9}{16}$	$\frac{15}{16}$	$\frac{15}{16}$	$\frac{7}{64}$	$4\frac{1}{2}$
8	33	$1\frac{7}{8}$	$\frac{9}{16}$	$\frac{9}{16}$	8	8	13	13	13	13	$\frac{9}{16}$	$\frac{9}{16}$	$\frac{15}{16}$	$\frac{15}{16}$	$\frac{3}{32}$	6

Table of link motion, taken from an engine cylinder 15 inches diameter; stroke 24 inches; steam-ports 14x1⅛ inches; exhaust-ports 14x2¼ inches; throw of eccentric 4 inches; lead ⅜ inch, in full stroke; centre of stud on saddle ⅛ inch back of centre line of link, toward axle; outside lap ⅜ inch on each end of valve; face of valve being ¾ inch longer than the total distance between the outside edges of steam-ports, inside having no lap; the width of cavity, or throat of valve, the total distance between the inner edges of steam-ports, rocker-shaft being used.

piston is worked expansively, from the fourth to the eighth notch. We also find the same difficulty as that shown in Table No. 1, by premature or too early lead, as we find, by referring to Table, that lead commences 1⅛ inches from end of stroke, when working in the fourth notch, and 1½ inches from end of stroke, when cutting off at half-stroke, or working in the sixth notch; and when working in the eighth notch, or cutting off at 8 inches, one-third of the stroke, premature lead takes place 3 inches from end of stroke, causing a counter-pressure that would be a difficult matter to overcome, without the increasing of lap, when giving lead for the full-stroke notch.

TABLE No. 3.—Taken from the same engine as that of Table No. 2, with the lead increased to ⅜ inch, in full-stroke, we therefore learn from Table No. 3, by increasing the lead, lessens the period of expansion, and hastens compression, and increases premature, or too early lead. By referring to this table, when cutting off at half-stroke, we find that premature lead has increased over one hundred per cent. above that shown in Table No. 2; and, when cutting off at one-third of the stroke, we also find one hundred per cent. of increase of premature lead, showing that lead is not to be allowed, as it creates a terrible counter-pressure by the premature or too early admission of steam, which rapidly increases with lead, as is shown by the tables.

VALVE TABLE OF LINK MOTION—NO. IV.

Notches.	Per cent. of admission.	Travel of valve.	Opening of Steam Port		Steam Cuts off. Expansion begins,		Exhaust Opens.		Exhaust closes, and Compression begins		Lead on Steam Port		Lead on Exhaust.		Slip of Link.	Lead commences from end of stroke
			Front Stroke	Back Stroke	Front Stroke	Back Stroke	Front Stroke	Back Stroke	Front Stroke	Back Stroke	Front Stroke	Back Stroke	Front Stroke	Back Stroke		
		Inch.	Inch.	Inch.	Inch.	Inch.	Inch.	Inch.	Inch.	Inch.	Inch.	Inch.	Inch.	Inch.	Inch.	Inch.
1	88	$4\frac{1}{2}$	$1\frac{3}{4}$	$1\frac{5}{8}$	$21\frac{1}{8}$	$21\frac{1}{4}$	23	$22\frac{7}{8}$	23	$22\frac{7}{8}$	$\frac{5}{16}$	$\frac{5}{16}$	1	1	$\frac{3}{4}$	0
2	79	$3\frac{11}{16}$	$1\frac{1}{4}$	$1\frac{5}{16}$	19	$19\frac{1}{8}$	$21\frac{7}{8}$	$21\frac{7}{8}$	$21\frac{7}{8}$	$21\frac{7}{8}$	$\frac{7}{16}$	$\frac{7}{16}$	$1\frac{1}{16}$	$1\frac{1}{16}$	$\frac{7}{16}$	$\frac{1}{4}$
3	71	$3\frac{1}{8}$	1	1	17	$17\frac{1}{8}$	$20\frac{3}{4}$	$20\frac{3}{4}$	$20\frac{3}{4}$	$20\frac{3}{4}$	$\frac{1}{2}$	$\frac{1}{2}$	$1\frac{1}{8}$	$1\frac{1}{8}$	$\frac{3}{8}$	$\frac{5}{8}$
4	62	$2\frac{7}{8}$	$\frac{13}{16}$	$\frac{13}{16}$	15	15	$19\frac{1}{2}$	$19\frac{1}{2}$	$19\frac{1}{2}$	$19\frac{1}{2}$	$\frac{33}{64}$	$\frac{33}{64}$	$1\frac{9}{64}$	$1\frac{9}{64}$	$\frac{9}{32}$	$1\frac{1}{8}$
5	59	$2\frac{5}{8}$	$\frac{3}{4}$	$\frac{3}{4}$	$13\frac{1}{2}$	$13\frac{1}{2}$	$18\frac{1}{2}$	$18\frac{1}{2}$	$18\frac{1}{2}$	$18\frac{1}{2}$	$\frac{17}{32}$	$\frac{17}{32}$	$1\frac{5}{32}$	$1\frac{5}{32}$	$\frac{7}{32}$	$1\frac{1}{2}$
6	50	$2\frac{9}{16}$	$\frac{11}{16}$	$\frac{11}{16}$	12	12	17	17	17	17	$\frac{17}{32}$	$\frac{17}{32}$	$1\frac{5}{32}$	$1\frac{5}{32}$	$\frac{5}{32}$	2
7	41	$2\frac{3}{8}$	$\frac{5}{8}$	$\frac{5}{8}$	10	10	16	16	16	16	$\frac{17}{32}$	$\frac{17}{32}$	$1\frac{5}{32}$	$1\frac{5}{32}$	$\frac{1}{8}$	3
8	33	$2\frac{5}{16}$	$\frac{5}{8}$	$\frac{5}{8}$	8	$8\frac{1}{8}$	$14\frac{1}{4}$	$14\frac{1}{4}$	$14\frac{1}{4}$	$14\frac{1}{4}$	$\frac{9}{16}$	$\frac{9}{16}$	$1\frac{3}{16}$	$1\frac{3}{16}$	$\frac{3}{32}$	4

Table of Link Motion, cylinder 16 inches diameter; stroke 24 inches; steam-ports 14 x 1¼ inches; exhaust 14 x 2½ inches; throw of eccentric 4½ inches; lead 5-16 inch, in full stroke; centre of stud on saddle 3-32 inch back of centre line of link, toward axle; outside lap ⅝ inch on each end of valve, face of valve being 1¼ inches longer than the extreme distance between outside edges of steam-ports, inside having no lap, the cavity or throat of valve being the same width as the distance between the inner edges of steam-ports; rocker-shaft being used.

TABLE NO. 4.—Diameter of cylinder 16 inches; stroke 24 inches; throw of eccentric 4½ inches; lap of valve ⅝ inch on each end, length of valve-face being 1¼ inches longer than the total distance between the outside edges of steam-ports, inside having no lap; the width of throat, or cavity of valve, being the same length as the distance between the inside edges of steam-ports. This table shows the effect of $\frac{5}{16}$ inch lead, in full stroke, with ⅝ inch lap. In referring back to Tables No's 2 and 3, we find that the distribution of steam, in Table No. 4, is a little better than Table No. 3, and not so good as Table No. 2, as the period of expansion is lessened six per cent. and compression hastened sixteen per cent. earlier in the stroke; and premature, or early lead, is increased twenty-seven per cent. earlier than is shown in Table No. 2. It is easily to be seen that lead, in all cases, creates a counter-pressure, by premature admission of steam, and lessens the period of expansion, and hastens compression; it also makes the period of expansion nearly the same quantity, from the fourth to the eighth notch.

TABLE NO. 5.—Diameter of cylinder 16 inches; stroke 24 inches; throw of eccentric 5 inches; lap of valve ⅞ inch on each end of valve; length of valve-face 1¾ inches longer than the extreme distance between the outside edges of steam-port; inside lap ⅛ inch on each end of valve; throat, or cavity of valve being ¼ inch narrower than distance between inner edges of steam-ports; lead, in full-stroke, $\frac{3}{16}$ inch, forward motion; back motion ⅛ inch less than none, rocker-shaft is used. This valve gives a fair table,

VALVE TABLE OF LINK MOTION—NO. V.

Notches.	Per cent. of admission.	Travel of valve.	Opening of Steam Port		Steam Cuts off. Expansion begins,		Exhaust Opens.		Exhaust closes, and Compression begins.		Lead on Steam Port		Lead on Exhaust.		Slip of Link.	Lead commences from end of stroke
			Front Stroke	Back Stroke	Front Stroke	Back Stroke	Front Stroke	Back Stroke	Front Stroke	Back Stroke	Front Stroke	Back Stroke	Front Stroke	Back Stroke		
		Inch.	Inch.	Inch.	Inch.	Inch.	Inch.	Inch.	Inch.	Inch.	Inch.	Inch.	Inch.	Inch.	Inch.	Inch.
1	84	5	$1\frac{5}{8}$	$1\frac{3}{4}$	$20\frac{1}{4}$	$20\frac{1}{2}$	$23\frac{1}{8}$	$23\frac{1}{4}$	$22\frac{1}{2}$	$22\frac{5}{8}$	$\frac{3}{16}$	$\frac{3}{16}$	$\frac{15}{16}$	$\frac{15}{16}$	$\frac{15}{16}$	0
2	79	$4\frac{3}{8}$	$1\frac{3}{16}$	$1\frac{1}{4}$	19	$19\frac{1}{4}$	$22\frac{5}{8}$	$22\frac{3}{4}$	22	22	$\frac{1}{4}$	$\frac{1}{4}$	1	1	$\frac{11}{16}$	0
3	71	$3\frac{13}{16}$	1	$1\frac{1}{32}$	17	$17\frac{1}{8}$	22	22	21	21	$\frac{9}{32}$	$\frac{9}{32}$	$1\frac{1}{32}$	$1\frac{1}{32}$	$\frac{1}{2}$	$\frac{1}{16}$
4	62	$3\frac{5}{16}$	$\frac{3}{4}$	$\frac{3}{4}$	15	15	$21\frac{1}{2}$	$21\frac{1}{2}$	$19\frac{3}{4}$	$19\frac{3}{4}$	$\frac{5}{16}$	$\frac{5}{16}$	$1\frac{1}{16}$	$1\frac{1}{16}$	$\frac{3}{8}$	$\frac{1}{4}$
5	59	$3\frac{1}{16}$	$\frac{11}{16}$	$\frac{11}{16}$	$13\frac{1}{2}$	$13\frac{1}{2}$	$20\frac{1}{2}$	$20\frac{1}{2}$	19	19	$\frac{5}{16}$	$\frac{5}{16}$	$1\frac{1}{16}$	$1\frac{1}{16}$	$\frac{5}{16}$	$\frac{3}{8}$
6	50	$2\frac{7}{8}$	$\frac{5}{8}$	$\frac{5}{8}$	12	12	$19\frac{3}{4}$	$19\frac{3}{4}$	18	18	$\frac{5}{16}$	$\frac{5}{16}$	$1\frac{1}{16}$	$1\frac{1}{16}$	$\frac{9}{32}$	$\frac{9}{16}$
7	41	$2\frac{3}{4}$	$\frac{1}{2}$	$\frac{1}{2}$	10	10	$18\frac{3}{4}$	$18\frac{3}{4}$	17	$16\frac{7}{8}$	$\frac{5}{16}$	$\frac{5}{16}$	$1\frac{1}{16}$	$1\frac{1}{16}$	$\frac{7}{32}$	$\frac{3}{4}$
8	33	$2\frac{5}{8}$	$\frac{7}{16}$	$\frac{7}{16}$	8	$8\frac{1}{16}$	$17\frac{3}{4}$	$17\frac{3}{4}$	$15\frac{3}{4}$	$15\frac{5}{8}$	$\frac{5}{16}$	$\frac{5}{16}$	$1\frac{1}{16}$	$1\frac{1}{16}$	$\frac{5}{32}$	$1\frac{1}{8}$

Table of Link Motion, cylinder 16 inches diameter; stroke 24 inches; steam-ports 14 x $1\frac{1}{4}$ inches; exhaust ports 15 x $2\frac{1}{2}$ inches; throw of eccentric 5 inches; lead 3-16 inch, in full stroke, forward motion; back motion blind having $\frac{1}{2}$ inch less than no lead in full stroke; centre of saddle stud $\frac{1}{8}$ inch back of centre line of link, toward axle; outside lap $\frac{7}{8}$ inch on each end of valve, face of valve being $1\frac{1}{4}$ inches longer than the distance between outside edges of steam-ports, inside having no lap, the cavity or throat of valve being $\frac{1}{4}$ inch narrower than the distance between the inner edges of steam-ports; a rocker-shaft being used.

the distribution of steam is good; the perfection of the motion consists in the nicety with which its motion is timed, relatively, with the motion of the piston. The movement of the piston is absolutely dependent upon the proper timing of the admission and release or exhausting of the steam. We cannot get a perfect motion, as we have the back pressure or compression to contend with, if we give clearance to overcome the compression, that is, to widen the throat or cavity of valve, to overcome the compression; the consequence, then, the loss will be greater than the gain, as the release or exhaust will take place too early in the stroke, which will be a loss of power and a waste of fuel. It will be observed, by referring to Table No. 5, showing, that when lead is increased in the forward motion, and the lead taken off the back motion, as in this case, the increase of lead will be less, when changing the engine from full-stroke to mid-gear. As will be seen, by looking over the table, that we have about the same lead, when working in the eighth notch, or cutting off at one-third of the stroke, as when set with $\frac{1}{16}$ inch lead for forward and back motion.

TABLE No. 6.—It will be observed, by referring to this table, which is the same motion, taken from the same engine as Table No. 5, except the lead, it being $\frac{1}{16}$ inch for forward and back stroke, showing that there is no particular gain received by increasing the lead for the forward motion, and decreasing the lead of the back motion, as is done on engine of Table No.

VALVE TABLE OF LINK MOTION.—NO. VI.

Notches.	Per cent of admission.	Travel of valve.	Opening of Steam Port		Steam cuts off. Expansion begins.		Exhaust Opens.		Exhaust closes, and compression begins.		Lead on Steam Port		Lead on Exhaust.		Slip of link.	Lead commences from end of stroke
			Front Stroke	Back Stroke	Front Stroke	Back Stroke	Front Stroke	Back Stroke	Front Stroke	Back Stroke	Front Stroke	Back Stroke	Front Stroke	Back Stroke		
		Inch.	Inch.	Inch.	Inch.	Inch.	Inch.	Inch.	Inch.	Inch.	Inch.	Inch.	Inch.	Inch.	Inch.	Inch
1	89	5	1 13/16	1 11/16	21 1/4	21 3/4	23 3/8	23 1/2	22 7/8	23	1/16	1/16	13/16	13/16	15/16	0
2	79	4 1/16	1 1/4	1 3/16	19	19 1/4	22 3/4	22 7/8	22	22 1/8	1/8	1/8	7/8	7/8	11/16	1/16
3	71	3 1/2	7/8	7/8	17	17 1/8	21 1/8	21 1/4	21	21 1/16	3/16	3/16	15/16	15/16	1/2	1/8
4	62	3 1/8	3/4	3/4	15	15	21 3/8	21 3/8	20	20	1/4	1/4	1	1	3/8	1/4
5	59	2 15/16	5/8	5/8	13 1/2	13 1/2	20 3/4	20 3/4	19 1/4	19 1/4	1/4	1/4	1	1	1/4	5/16
6	50	2 3/4	1/2	1/2	12	12	20	20	18 3/8	18 3/8	1/4	1/4	1	1	3/16	7/16
7	41	2 5/8	13/32	13/32	10	10	19	19	17 1/16	17	17/64	17/64	1 1/64	1 1/64	3/16	11/16
8	33	2 3/8	11/32	11/32	8	8	18	18	15 7/8	15 3/4	9/32	9/32	1 1/32	1 1/32	3/16	15/16

Table of link motion, cylinder 16 inches diameter; stroke 24 inches; steam-ports 15x1¼ inches; exhaust-ports 15x2¼ inches; throw of eccentric 5 inches; lead 1-16 inch, in full stroke; centre of saddle stud ⅛ inch back of centre line of link, toward axle; outside lap ⅞ inch on each end of valve; face of valve being 1¾ inches longer than the extreme distance between the outside edges of steam-ports; inside lap ⅛ inch on each end; the cavity, or throat of valve being ¼ inch narrower than the distance between the inner edges of steam-ports, rocker-shaft being used.

5, as both tables show about the same distribution of steam, except in full-stroke notch. There is a gain in favor of engine of Table No. 5, as it shows that the release or exhaust takes place a little sooner, which is of importance at this point. When working in full-stroke this gain will be overcome by the absence of lead, when working the engine in back motion, as there will not be any lead in back motion, from the first to the third notch, until the piston has passed the centre; the remaining notches will have sufficient lead.

TABLES No's 7 and 8.—Showing the effect of inside lap; cylinder 16 inches; stroke 24 inches; throw of eccentric 5 inches; lap 1 inch on each end of valve, face of valve being 2 inches longer than the total distance between the outside edges of steam-port; insides lap ¼ inch on each end of valve; the throat or cavity of valve being ½ inch narrower than the distance between inner edges of steam-ports.

TABLE No. 8 having no inside lap, throat or cavity of valve being the same distance between the inner edges of steam-ports. By referring to Tables 7 and 8, we find that both tables show nearly the same percentage of release and compression, from the beginning of the stroke, tor the full-stroke notch. Table No. 7, with ¼ inch inside lap, shows, that when working in the sixth, or half-stroke notch, that release takes place seven per cent. later in the stroke, and that compression begins seven per cent. earlier, from the beginning of the stroke, than is shown in Table No.

VALVE TABLE OF LINK MOTION—NO. VII.

Notches.	Per cent. of admission.	Travel of valve.	Opening of Steam Port		Steam cuts off, Expansion begins.		Exhaust Opens.		Exhaust closes, and compression begins.		Lead on Steam Port		Lead on Exhaust.		Slip of Link	Lead commences from end of stroke
			Front Stroke	Back Stroke	Front Stroke	Back Stroke	Front Stroke	Back Stroke	Front Stroke	Back Stroke	Front Stroke	Back Stroke	Front Stroke	Back Stroke		
		Inch.	Inch.	Inch.	Inch.	Inch.	Inch.	Inch.	Inch.	Inch.	Inch.	Inch.	Inch.	Inch.	Inch.	Inch.
1	83	$4\frac{15}{16}$	$1\frac{5}{8}$	$1\frac{7}{16}$	$19\frac{7}{8}$	$20\frac{1}{16}$	$22\frac{7}{16}$	$23\frac{5}{16}$	$23\frac{3}{8}$	$23\frac{5}{16}$	$\frac{1}{16}$	$\frac{1}{16}$	$\frac{13}{16}$	$\frac{13}{16}$	$\frac{15}{16}$	0
2	79	$4\frac{9}{16}$	$1\frac{3}{8}$	$1\frac{1}{4}$	19	$19\frac{3}{16}$	$23\frac{3}{16}$	$23\frac{1}{8}$	$21\frac{7}{8}$	$21\frac{7}{8}$	$\frac{1}{8}$	$\frac{1}{8}$	$\frac{7}{8}$	$\frac{7}{8}$	$\frac{3}{4}$	0
3	71	$3\frac{11}{16}$	1	$\frac{15}{16}$	17	$17\frac{1}{8}$	$22\frac{5}{8}$	$22\frac{5}{8}$	$20\frac{3}{4}$	$20\frac{3}{4}$	$\frac{3}{16}$	$\frac{3}{16}$	$\frac{15}{16}$	$\frac{15}{16}$	$\frac{9}{16}$	$\frac{1}{16}$
4	62	$3\frac{1}{2}$	$\frac{3}{4}$	$\frac{23}{33}$	15	15	22	22	$19\frac{5}{8}$	$19\frac{5}{8}$	$\frac{7}{32}$	$\frac{7}{32}$	$\frac{31}{32}$	$\frac{31}{32}$	$\frac{7}{16}$	$\frac{1}{8}$
5	59	$3\frac{5}{16}$	$\frac{11}{16}$	$\frac{11}{16}$	$13\frac{1}{2}$	$13\frac{1}{2}$	$21\frac{1}{2}$	$21\frac{3}{8}$	$18\frac{9}{16}$	$18\frac{5}{8}$	$\frac{1}{4}$s	$\frac{1}{4}$s	1s	1s	$\frac{3}{8}$	$\frac{3}{16}$
6	50	$3\frac{1}{8}$	$\frac{1}{2}$	$\frac{1}{2}$	12	12	$20\frac{3}{4}$	$20\frac{5}{8}$	18	$17\frac{7}{8}$	$\frac{1}{4}$s	$\frac{1}{4}$s	1s	1s	$\frac{5}{16}$	$\frac{5}{16}$
7	41	$2\frac{15}{16}$	$\frac{7}{16}$	$\frac{7}{16}$	10	10	20	$19\frac{15}{16}$	$16\frac{5}{8}$	$16\frac{1}{2}$	$\frac{1}{4}$	$\frac{1}{4}$	1	1	$\frac{1}{4}$	$\frac{1}{2}$
8	33	$2\frac{3}{4}$	$\frac{3}{8}$	$\frac{3}{8}$	8	8	19	19	$15\frac{1}{8}$	15	$\frac{1}{4}$	$\frac{1}{4}$	1	1	$\frac{3}{16}$	$\frac{3}{4}$

Table of link motion, cylinder 16 inches diameter; stroke 24 inches; steam-ports 15x1¼ inches; exhaust-ports 15x2½ inches; throw of eccentric 4 inches; lead 1-16 inch, in full stroke; centre of saddle stud 3-32 inch back of centre line of link, toward axle; outside lap 1 inch on each end of valve, face of valve being 2 inches longer than the distance between the outside edges of steam-port, inside lap ¼ inch on each end; the throat or cavity of valve being ½ inch narrower than the distance between the inner edges of steam-ports, rocker-shaft being used.

8, with no inside lap. Table No. 7 shows, when working in the eighth notch, or cutting off at one-third of the stroke, with $\frac{1}{4}$ inch inside lap, that release takes place eight per cent later in the stroke, and compression begins eight per cent. earlier, from beginning of stroke, than is shown in table No. 8, with no inside lap; showing that inside lap prolongs expansion, and likewise increases the period of compression, to the same extent that release is deferred.

TABLES No's 9 and 10.—Showing the effects produced by increasing the throw of the eccentric. Table No. 9 showing the effect of $4\frac{1}{2}$ inches throw of eccentric; Table No. 10 showing the effect of $6\frac{1}{4}$ inches throw of eccentric. Both tables were taken from the same engine, cylinder 16 inches in diameter; stroke 22 inches; outside lap $\frac{3}{4}$ inch, on each end of valve, making the valve-face $1\frac{1}{2}$ inches longer than the total distance between the outside edges of steam-ports; inside has no lap, or line-and-line, as it is termed; the throat, or cavity of valve being the same width as the distance between the inner edges of steam-ports; lead $\frac{1}{16}$ inch in full-stroke. By referring to the tables, we find very little difference in the distribution of steam, as both tables show about the same, for the four points of distribution: admission, expansion, compression, and release or exhaust, takes place at the same time in both tables. Table No. 10 shows again in favor of $6\frac{1}{4}$ inch throw of eccentric, by the increase of lead and opening of steam-ports; as Table No. 10 shows an average of twenty per cent.

VALVE TABLE OF LINK MOTION—NO. VIII.

Notches.	Per cent. of admission.	Travel of valve.	Opening of Steam Port		Steam cuts off, Expansion begins.		Exhaust Opens.		Exhaust closes, and compression begins.		Lead on Steam Port		Lead on Exhaust.		Slip of Link	Lead commences from end of stroke
			Front Stroke	Back Stroke	Front Stroke	Back Stroke	Front Stroke	Back Stroke	Front Stroke	Back Stroke	Front Stroke	Back Stroke	Front Stroke	Back Stroke		
		Inch.	Inch.	Inch.	Inch.	Inch.	Inch.	Inch.	Inch.	Inch.	Inch.	Inch.	Inch.	Inch.	Inch.	Inch.
1	83	$4\frac{15}{16}$	$1\frac{5}{8}$	$1\frac{7}{16}$	$19\frac{7}{8}$	$20\frac{1}{16}$	23	$22\frac{15}{16}$	23	$22\frac{15}{16}$	$\frac{1}{16}$	$\frac{1}{16}$	$\frac{13}{16}$	$\frac{13}{16}$	$\frac{15}{16}$	0
2	79	$4\frac{9}{16}$	$1\frac{3}{8}$	$1\frac{1}{4}$	19	$19\frac{3}{16}$	$22\frac{5}{8}$	$22\frac{5}{8}$	$22\frac{5}{8}$	$22\frac{5}{8}$	$\frac{1}{8}$	$\frac{1}{8}$	$\frac{7}{8}$	$\frac{7}{8}$	$\frac{3}{4}$	0
3	71	$3\frac{11}{16}$	1	$\frac{15}{16}$	17	$17\frac{1}{8}$	$21\frac{5}{8}$	$21\frac{5}{8}$	$21\frac{5}{8}$	$21\frac{5}{8}$	$\frac{3}{16}$	$\frac{3}{16}$	$\frac{15}{16}$	$\frac{15}{16}$	$\frac{9}{16}$	$\frac{1}{16}$
4	62	$3\frac{1}{2}$	$\frac{3}{4}$	$\frac{3}{4}$	15	15	$20\frac{3}{4}$	$20\frac{3}{4}$	$20\frac{3}{4}$	$20\frac{3}{4}$	$\frac{7}{32}$	$\frac{7}{32}$	$\frac{31}{32}$	$\frac{31}{32}$	$\frac{7}{16}$	$\frac{1}{8}$
5	59	$3\frac{5}{16}$	$\frac{11}{16}$	$\frac{11}{16}$	$13\frac{1}{2}$	$13\frac{1}{2}$	$20\frac{1}{8}$	$20\frac{1}{8}$	$20\frac{1}{8}$	$20\frac{1}{8}$	$\frac{1}{4}$	$\frac{1}{4}$	1	1	$\frac{3}{8}$	$\frac{3}{16}$
6	50	$3\frac{1}{8}$	$\frac{1}{2}$	$\frac{1}{2}$	12	12	$19\frac{1}{2}$	$19\frac{1}{2}$	$19\frac{1}{2}$	$19\frac{1}{2}$	$\frac{1}{4}$	$\frac{1}{4}$	1	1	$\frac{5}{16}$	$\frac{5}{16}$
7	41	$2\frac{15}{16}$	$\frac{7}{16}$	$\frac{7}{16}$	10	10	$18\frac{1}{2}$	$18\frac{1}{2}$	$18\frac{1}{2}$	$18\frac{1}{2}$	$\frac{1}{4}$	$\frac{1}{4}$	1	1	$\frac{1}{4}$	$\frac{1}{2}$
8	33	$2\frac{3}{4}$	$\frac{3}{8}$	$\frac{3}{8}$	8	8	$17\frac{1}{4}$	$17\frac{1}{4}$	$17\frac{1}{4}$	$17\frac{1}{4}$	$\frac{1}{4}$	$\frac{1}{4}$	1	1	$\frac{3}{16}$	$\frac{3}{4}$

Table of link motion, cylinder 16 inches diameter; stroke 24 inches; steam-ports 15x1¼ inches; exhaust-ports 15x2½ inches; throw of eccentric 5 inches; lead 1-16 inch, in full stroke; centre of saddle stud 3-32 inch back of centre line of link, toward axle; outside lap 1 inch on each end of valve, face of valve being 2 inches longer than the total distance between the outside edges of steam-ports, inside having no lap, the cavity or throat of valve being the same width as the distance between inner edges of steam-ports, rocker-shaft being used.

more lead, for all the notches, from the third to the eighth notch, and a less wire-drawing of steam, as the opening of steam-port averages ten per cent. more opening, from the first to the sixth notch, than is shown in Table No. 9. The seventh and eighth notches show the same for both tables. We also find a loss of power, by counter-pressure, produced by the increasing of fifty per cent. of premature or too early lead; consequently, the counter-pressure will give greater resistance than will be gained by the increasing of opening of steam-port. We also find, by increasing the throw of the eccentric to 6¼ inches, that we have increased the slip of link about sixty per cent. above that produced by the 4½ inch throw of eccentric, as will be seen by referring to the tables. We find, by increasing the throw of eccentric, it also changes the location of the centre of stud on saddle, causing it to move horizontally toward the axle, which causes the increase of slip of link. The location of centre of stud on saddle, for the 4½ inch throw of eccentric, being $\frac{3}{16}$ inch back of centre line of link, toward axle, the 6¼ inch throw of eccentric being ⅜ inch back of centre line of link, toward axle, and in the middle of the length of link. All saddles are generally placed in the centre of the length of link.

TABLES No's 11 and 12.—Showing the effect produced on the same engine, by moving the point of suspension less than ¼ inch. Cylinder 16 inches in diameter: stroke 22 inches; throw of eccentrics 4½ inches; lead ⅛ inch in full-stroke; outside lap ⅝ inch

VALVE TABLE OF LINK MOTION.—NO. IX.

Notches.	Per cent of admission.	Travel of valve.	Opening of Steam Port		Steam cuts off. Expansion begins.		Exhaust Opens.		Exhaust closes, and compression begins.		Lead on Steam Port		Lead on Exhaust.		Slip of link.	Lead commences from end of stroke
			Front Stroke	Back Stroke	Front Stroke	Back Stroke	Front Stroke	Back Stroke	Front Stroke	Back Stroke	Front Stroke	Back Stroke	Front Stroke	Back Stroke		
		Inch.	Inch.	Inch.	Inch.	Inch.	Inch.	Inch.	Inch.	Inch.	Inch.	Inch.	Inch.	Inch.	Inch.	Inch,
1	91	4 1/2	1 9/16	1 1/2	19 3/8	19 5/8	21 3/8	21 3/8	21 3/8	21 3/8	1/16	1/16	13/16	13/16	7/8	0
2	82	3 7/8	1 1/4	1 5/32	18	18 1/4	20 3/4	20 3/4	20 3/4	20 3/4	1/8	1/8	7/8	7/8	5/8	0
3	73	3 1/4	29/32	7/8	16	16 3/16	20	20	20	20	7/32	7/32	1 3/32	1 3/32	7/16	1/16
4	63	2 3/4	5/8	5/8	14	14 1/16	19	19	19	19	1/4	1/4	1 1/8	1 1/8	3/8	3/16
5	56	2 9/16	9/16	9/16	12 1/2	12 1/2	18 3/16	18 1/4	18 3/16	18 1/4	1/4	1/4	1 1/8	1 1/8	1/4	5/16
6	50	2 7/16	1/2	1/2	11	11	17 3/8	17 1/2	17 3/8	17 1/2	1/4	1/4	1 1/8	1 1/8	15/64	1/2
7	41	2 9/32	7/16	7/16	9	9	16 1/2	16 1/4	16 1/4	16 1/4	1/4	1/4	1 1/8	1 1/8	3/16	3/4
8	32	2 3/16	3/8	3/8	7	7	14 7/8	14 7/8	14 7/8	14 7/8	17/64	17/64	1 9/64	1 9/64	1/8	1 1/8

Table of link motion, cylinder 16 inches diameter; stroke 22 inches; steam-ports 15x1⅛ inches; exhaust-ports 15x2½ inches; throw of eccentric 4½ inches; lead 1-16 inch, in full stroke; centre of stud on saddle ⅛ inch back of centre line of link, toward axle; outside lap ¾ inch on each end of valve; inside having no lap being line and line; the throat of valve being the same width as the distance between the inner edges of steam-ports, rocker-shaft being used.

on each end of valve, face of valve being 1½ inches longer than the extreme distance between outside edges of steam-ports, inside having no lap; the cavity or throat of valve being the same width as the distance between the inner edges of steam-ports, rock-shaft being used. Referring to Table No. 11, the point of suspension, or the locating the centre of stud on saddle $\frac{3}{32}$ of an inch back of centre line of link, toward axle, it will be observed that the value of the back stroke admission of steam is greatest; while the opening of steam-port, for front stroke, is greater than the opening of steam-port, for back stroke. It will be observed, also, that exhaust and compression take place on the front stroke sooner than on the back stroke, which is the reverse to that shown on Valve Table No. 12, with point of suspension or centre of saddle-stud located ⅛ inch forward of centre line of link toward cylinder; which shows the greatest value of admission of steam is given on the front stroke, and opening of steam-port greatest on the back stroke; and the exhaust and compression takes place earlier on the back stroke, *vice versa* from that shown on Table No. 11, showing clearly that the proper place for the location of the centre of stud on saddle would be, for this particular motion, about on the centre line of link. It will also be observed that both tables show about the same distribution of steam, in full-stroke; while changing from full-stroke to half-stroke, and mid-gear, the change of motion takes place, showing the quality of the link motion derived from the lo-

VALVE TABLE OF LINK MOTION—NO. X.

Notches.	Per cent. of admission.	Travel of valve.	Opening of Steam Port		Steam Cuts off. Expansion begins,		Exhaust Opens.		Exhaust closes, and Compression begins		Lead on Steam Port		Lead on Exhaust.		Slip of Link.	Lead commences from end of stroke
			Front Stroke	Back Stroke	Front Stroke	Back Stroke	Front Stroke	Back Stroke	Front Stroke	Back Stroke	Front Stroke	Back Stroke	Front Stroke	Back Stroke		
		Inch.	Inch.	Inch.	Inch.	Inch.	Inch.	Inch.	Inch.	Inch.	Inch.	Inch.	Inch.	Inch.	Inch.	Inch.
1	91	6 3/16	2 3/8	2 1/4	20 1/8	20 1/2	21 1/2	21 5/8	21 1/2	21 5/8	1/16	1/16	13/16	13/16	1 1/8	0
2	82	4 5/32	1 3/8	1 15/16	18	18 1/4	20 1/2	20 9/16	20 1/2	20 9/16	7/32	7/32	1 1/32	1 1/32	15/16	1/8
3	73	3 5/16	15/16	7/8	16	16 1/16	19 1/2	19 1/2	19 1/2	19 1/2	9/32	9/32	1 3/32	1 3/32	13/16	1/4
4	63	2 7/8	11/16	11/16	14	14	18 3/4	18 3/4	18 3/4	18 3/4	5/16	5/16	1 1/16	1 1/16	9/16	3/8
5	56	2 11/16	5/8	5/8	12 1/2	12 1/2	17 7/8	17 7/8	17 7/8	17 7/8	5/16	5/16	1 1/16	1 1/16	1/2	5/8
6	50	2 1/2	17/32	17/32	11	10 7/8	17 1/16	17 1/16	17 1/16	17 1/16	5/16	5/16	1 1/16	1 1/16	7/16	7/8
7	41	2 3/8	7/16	7/16	9	8 15/16	16 1/8	16 1/8	16 1/8	16 1/8	21/64	21/64	1 5/64	1 5/64	13/32	1 1/8
8	32	2 1/4	3/8	3/8	7	7	14 5/8	14 5/8	14 5/8	14 5/8	11/32	11/32	1 3/32	1 3/32	3/8	1 1/2

Table of Link Motion, cylinder 16 inches diameter; stroke 22 inches; steam-ports 15x 1¼ inches; exhaust ports, 15 x 2½ inches; throw of eccentric 6¼ inches; lead 1-16 inch, in full stroke; centre of stud on saddle ¾ inch back of centre line of link, toward axle; outside lap ¾ inch on each end of valve, face of valve being 1½ inches longer than the extreme distance between outside edges of steam-ports, inside having no lap, the cavity or throat of valve being the same width as the distance between the inner edges of steam-ports; a rocker-shaft being used.

cating the centre of stud on saddle of link, or point of suspension, as it is termed. The point of suspension being the most important of all the working centres, in regard to equalizing the cut-off or regulating the distribution of steam.

TABLE No. 13.—Showing the effect of transferring the motion of Valve Table No. 11 to a 24-inch stroke engine, by lengthening the crank and main rod to their proper lengths; the eccentrics and eccentric-rods were not disturbed. Table No. 11 being a 22-inch stroke engine, the length of connecting-rod being 77 inches, or 3½ times the length of stroke; the length of connecting-rod of Valve Table No. 13, 84 inches, being the proper length for a 24-inch stroke engine, being 3½ times the length of stroke. It will be observed, by referring to Table No. 13, that the location of centre of saddle stud $\frac{3}{32}$ of an inch back of centre-line of link, towards axle, is the proper place for this motion, as the table shows that an equal distribution of steam takes place for admission, expansion, release and compression for the front and back stroke, also an equal opening ot steam-port. We also learn, from Valve Tables No's 11 and 13, the distribution derived from the link, is affected slightly by the length of connecting-rod and throw of crank; as we find, by lengthening the crank 2 inches, and connecting-rod 7 inches, we have gained an increase for the front stroke, and less admission of steam for the back stroke, than that shown in Table No. 11, with a shorter connecting-rod and crank; the eccentrics required the same position

VALVE TABLE OF LINK MOTION—NO. XI.

Notches.	Per cent. of admission.	Travel of valve.	Opening of Steam Port		Steam Cuts off. Expansion begins,		Exhaust Opens.		Exhaust closes, and Compression begins		Lead on Steam Port		Lead on Exhaust.		Slip of Link.	Lead commences from end of stroke
			Front Stroke	Back Stroke	Front Stroke	Back Stroke	Front Stroke	Back Stroke	Front Stroke	Back Stroke	Front Stroke	Back Stroke	Front Stroke	Back Stroke		
		Inch.	Inch.	Inch.	Inch.	Inch.	Inch.	Inch.	Inch.	Inch.	Inch.	Inch.	Inch.	Inch.	Inch.	Inch.
1	90	4 1/2	1 11/16	1 9/16	19 7/8	20 1/8	21 3/8	21 1/2	21 3/8	21 1/2	1/8	1/8	3/4	3/4	13/16	0
2	77	3 1/8	1	31/32	17	17 3/8	20 1/8	20 1/4	20 1/8	20 1/4	7/32	7/32	27/32	27/32	3/8	1/8
3	71	2 11/16	23/32	11/16	15	15 3/8	19 1/8	19 3/8	19 1/8	19 3/8	1/4	9/32	7/8	29/32	5/16	5/16
4	59	2 3/8	9/16	17/32	13	13 3/16	18 1/8	18 1/2	18 1/8	18 1/2	19/64	5/16	29/32	15/16	1/4	1/2
5	50	2 3/16	1/2	15/32	11	11 1/8	17	17 1/4	17	17 1/4	5/16	5/16	15/16	15/16	3/16	1
6	41	2 1/16	13/32	25/64	9	9 1/8	16	16	16	16	5/16	5/16	15/16	15/16	1/8	1 3/8
7	33	1 15/16	3/8	11/32	7	7 1/4	14 3/8	14 1/4	14 3/8	14 1/4	11/32	11/32	15/16	15/16	3/32	2

Table of Link Motion, cylinder 16 inches diameter; stroke 22 inches; steam-ports 14x 1 1/4 inches; exhaust ports, 14 x 2 1/2 inches; throw of eccentric 4 1/2 inches; lead 1-8 inch, in full stroke centre of stud on saddle 3-32 inch back of centre line of link, toward axle; outside lap 5/8 inch on each end of valve, face of valve being 1 1/4 inches longer than the extreme distance between outside edges of steam-ports, inside having no lap, the cavity or throat of valve being the same width as the distance between the inner edges of steam-ports; a rocker-shaft being used.

on the axle for both engines, also the same length of eccentric-rods precisely; therefore, the term link motion, so far as it involves the relation of the valve motion to that of the connecting-rod and crank, includes the proportion of the piston motion.

TABLES No's 14 and 15.—Taken from the same engine, showing the effect produced by increasing the horizontal distance between the centre of knuckle-joints and centre line of link, toward axle, to 4 inches, being 1½ inches more than is generally given; cylinder 16 inches in diameter; stroke 24 inches; throw of eccentric 5½ inches; lead ⅛ inch, in full stroke; centre of stud on saddle, of Table No. 14, 1 inch back of centre line of link; No. 15, ¼ inch back of centre line of link, toward axle; outside lap ¾ inch on each end of valve, face of valve being 1½ inches longer than the total distance between the outside edges of steam-ports; inside lap 1/16 inch on each end of valve, the cavity or throat of valve being ⅛ inch narrower than the distance between the inner edges of steam-ports; rock-shaft used. By referring to Table No. 14, we learn, by increasing the horizontal distance from 2½ inches to 4 inches, between the centre of knuckle-joint and centre line of link, toward axle, that it causes considerable change in the motion, as Table No. 14 shows an average increase of 70 per cent. of slip of link above that shown in Table No. 15, with knuckle-joint centres 2½ inches back of centre line of link, being 1½ inches less distance than that of Table No. 14. We also learn from Table No. 14, that prema-

VALVE TABLE OF LINK MOTION—NO. XII.

Notches.	Per cent. of admission.	Travel of valve.	Opening of Steam Port		Steam cuts off, Expansion begins.		Exhaust Opens.		Exhaust closes, and compression begins.		Lead on Steam Port		Lead on Exhaust.		Slip of Link	Lead commences from end of stroke
			Front Stroke	Back Stroke	Front Stroke	Back Stroke	Front Stroke	Back Stroke	Front Stroke	Back Stroke	Front Stroke	Back Stroke	Front Stroke	Back Stroke		
		Inch.	Inch.	Inch.	Inch.	Inch.	Inch.	Inch.	Inch.	Inch.	Inch.	Inch.	Inch.	Inch.	Inch.	Inch.
1	90	$4\frac{1}{2}$	$1\frac{11}{16}$	$1\frac{9}{16}$	$19\frac{3}{4}$	20	$21\frac{1}{4}$	$21\frac{3}{8}$	$21\frac{1}{4}$	$21\frac{3}{8}$	$\frac{1}{8}$	$\frac{1}{8}$	$\frac{3}{4}$	$\frac{3}{4}$	$\frac{3}{4}$	0
2	77	$3\frac{1}{8}$	$\frac{31}{32}$	$\frac{15}{16}$	17	17	$20\frac{1}{4}$	$20\frac{3}{16}$	$20\frac{1}{4}$	$20\frac{3}{16}$	$\frac{7}{32}$	$\frac{7}{32}$	$\frac{27}{32}$	$\frac{27}{32}$	$\frac{3}{8}$	$\frac{1}{8}$
3	71	$2\frac{11}{16}$	$\frac{11}{16}$	$\frac{23}{32}$	$15\frac{3}{8}$	$15\frac{1}{16}$	$19\frac{3}{8}$	$19\frac{1}{8}$	$19\frac{3}{8}$	$19\frac{1}{8}$	$\frac{9}{32}$	$\frac{1}{4}$	$\frac{29}{32}$	$\frac{29}{32}$	$\frac{5}{16}$	$\frac{5}{16}$
4	59	$2\frac{3}{8}$	$\frac{17}{32}$	$\frac{9}{16}$	$13\frac{3}{16}$	13	$18\frac{3}{8}$	$18\frac{1}{8}$	$18\frac{3}{8}$	$18\frac{1}{8}$	$\frac{5}{16}$	$\frac{9}{32}$	$\frac{15}{16}$	$\frac{15}{16}$	$\frac{1}{4}$	$\frac{1}{2}$
5	50	$2\frac{3}{16}$	$\frac{15}{32}$	$\frac{1}{2}$	$11\frac{1}{8}$	11	$17\frac{5}{16}$	17	$17\frac{5}{16}$	17	$\frac{5}{16}$	$\frac{5}{16}$	$\frac{15}{16}$	$\frac{15}{16}$	$\frac{3}{16}$	1
6	41	$2\frac{1}{16}$	$\frac{25}{64}$	$\frac{13}{32}$	$9\frac{1}{16}$	9	16	16	16	16	$\frac{5}{16}$	$\frac{5}{16}$	$\frac{15}{16}$	$\frac{15}{16}$	$\frac{1}{8}$	$1\frac{1}{2}$
7	32	2	$\frac{11}{32}$	$\frac{3}{8}$	$7\frac{1}{4}$	7	$14\frac{1}{8}$	$14\frac{3}{8}$	$14\frac{1}{8}$	$14\frac{3}{8}$	$\frac{11}{32}$	$\frac{11}{32}$	$\frac{31}{32}$	$\frac{31}{32}$	$\frac{3}{32}$	2

Table of link motion, cylinder 16 inches diameter; stroke 22 inches; steam-ports 14x1¼ inches; exhaust-ports 14x2½ inches; throw of eccentric 4½ inches; lead ⅛ inch, in full stroke; centre of stud on saddle ⅛ inch forward of centre line of link, toward cylinders; outside lap ⅝ inch on each end of valve, face of valve being 1¼ inches longer than the extreme distance between the outside edges of steam-ports, inside having no lap, the width of cavity or throat of valve being the same distance as between inner edges of steam-ports, rocker-shaft being used.

VALVE TABLE OF LINK MOTION.—NO. XIII.

Notches.	Per cent. of admission.	Travel of valve.	Opening of Steam Port		Steam cuts off. Expansion begins.		Exhaust Opens.		Exhaust closes, and compression begins.		Lead on Steam Port		Lead on Exhaust.		Slip of link.	Lead commences from end of stroke
			Front Stroke	Back Stroke	Front Stroke	Back Stroke	Front Stroke	Back Stroke	Front Stroke	Back Stroke	Front Stroke	Back Stroke	Front Stroke	Back Stroke		
		Inch.	Inch.	Inch.	Inch.	Inch.	Inch.	Inch.	Inch.	Inch.	Inch.	Inch.	Inch.	Inch.	Inch.	Inch,
1	91	4 1/2	1 5/8	1 1/2	21 3/4	21 7/8	23 3/8	23 1/4	23 3/8	23 1/4	1/8	1/8	3/4	3/4	3/4	0
2	79	3 1/4	1 1/16	1	19	19 1/8	22 1/4	22 1/8	22 1/4	22 1/8	1/4	1/4	7/8	7/8	7/16	1/16
3	71	2 3/16	25/32	3/4	17	17	21 1/4	21 1/4	21 1/4	21 1/4	5/16	5/16	15/16	15/16	3/8	3/8
4	62	2 1/2	11/16	11/16	15	15	20	20	20	20	5/16	5/16	15/16	15/16	5/16	5/8
5	59	2 3/8	9/16	9/16	13 1/2	13 1/2	19 1/2	19 1/2	19 1/2	19 1/2	5/16	5/16	15/16	15/16	1/4	7/8
6	50	2 1/4	1/2	1/2	12	12	18 1/2	18 1/2	18 1/2	18 1/2	5/16	5/16	15/16	15/16	3/16	1 1/8
7	41	2 1/8	13/32	13/32	10	10	17	17	17	17	5/16	5/16	15/16	15/16	1/8	1 5/8
8	33	2	3/8	3/8	8	8	15 1/4	15 1/8	15 1/4	15 1/8	21/64	21/64	31/32	31/32	3/32	2 3/8

Table of link motion, cylinder 16 inches diameter; stroke 24 inches; steam-ports 14x1¼ inches; exhaust-ports 14x2½ inches; throw of eccentric 4½ inches; lead ⅛ inch full stroke, centre of stud on saddle 3-32 back of centre line of link, toward axle; outside lap ⅝ inch on each end of valve; face of valve being 1¼ inches longer than the extreme distance between outer edges of steam ports; inside having no lap the cavity or throat of valve being the width of the distance between the inner edges of steam-ports, rocker-shafts being used.

ture or too early lead, takes place 54 per cent. earlier, on an average, from the fifth to the eighth notch, than is shown in Table No. 15, with 2½ inches distance between knuckle-joint centres and centre line of link, the location of centre of stud on saddle ¼ inch back of centre line of link, toward axle, and in centre of length of link, the valve receiving the same travel as the throw of eccentric; while that of Valve Table No. 14, with knuckle-joint centre 4 inches back of centre line of link, the valve receives $\frac{3}{16}$ inch less travel than the throw of the eccentric; also showing an average of 25 per cent. less opening of steam-port, which is caused by the centre of stud on saddle being located 1 inch back of centre line of link, toward axle. It will be observed the greater the distance the knuckle-joint centres are from the centre line of link the greater will be the distance of the locating of the centre of stud on saddle, in the same direction from the centre line of link, which will also cause a greater amount of slip of link on the block, and increase of premature or too early lead. We therefore learn, from Valve Tables No.'s 14 and 15, by increasing the horizontal distance 1½ inches more than the general rule, from the centre line of link, back toward axle, we meet with difficulties, in the shape of increase of slip of link, also premature lead, decrease of travel of valve, and also less opening of steam-port; while the admission, expansion, release, exhaust, and compression show no material change, both tables showing the same.

VALVE TABLE OF LINK MOTION.—NO. XIV.

Notches.	Per cent. of admission.	Travel of valve.	Opening of Steam Port		Steam cuts off. Expansion begins.		Exhaust Opens.		Exhaust closes, and compression begins.		Lead on Steam Port		Lead on Exhaust.		Slip of link.	Lead commences from end of stroke
			Front Stroke	Back Stroke	Front Stroke	Back Stroke	Front Stroke	Back Stroke	Front Stroke	Back Stroke	Front Stroke	Back Stroke	Front Stroke	Back Stroke		
		Inch.	Inch.	Inch.	Inch.	Inch.	Inch.	Inch.	Inch.	Inch.	Inch.	Inch.	Inch.	Inch.	Inch.	Inch,
1	90	$5\frac{5}{16}$	$1\frac{7}{8}$	$1\frac{3}{4}$	$21\frac{1}{2}$	$21\frac{5}{8}$	$23\frac{1}{2}$	$23\frac{3}{8}$	$23\frac{1}{4}$	$23\frac{1}{8}$	$\frac{1}{8}$	$\frac{1}{8}$	$\frac{13}{16}$	$\frac{13}{16}$	$1\frac{5}{8}$	0
2	79	$3\frac{3}{4}$	$1\frac{1}{8}$	$1\frac{3}{32}$	19	19	$22\frac{1}{2}$	$22\frac{3}{8}$	22	$21\frac{7}{8}$	$\frac{1}{4}$	$\frac{1}{4}$	$\frac{15}{16}$	$\frac{15}{16}$	$1\frac{1}{8}$	$\frac{1}{8}$
3	71	$3\frac{5}{16}$	$\frac{7}{8}$	$\frac{27}{32}$	17	17	$21\frac{3}{4}$	$21\frac{5}{8}$	21	$20\frac{7}{8}$	$\frac{17}{32}$	$\frac{17}{32}$	$\frac{31}{32}$	$\frac{31}{32}$	$\frac{15}{16}$	$\frac{3}{8}$
4	62	$2\frac{7}{8}$	$\frac{11}{16}$	$\frac{11}{16}$	15	15	$20\frac{3}{4}$	$20\frac{1}{2}$	20	$19\frac{3}{4}$	$\frac{5}{16}$	$\frac{5}{16}$	1	1	$\frac{13}{16}$	$\frac{5}{8}$
5	59	$2\frac{3}{4}$	$\frac{5}{8}$	$\frac{5}{8}$	$13\frac{1}{2}$	$13\frac{1}{2}$	$20\frac{1}{8}$	$19\frac{7}{8}$	$19\frac{3}{8}$	$18\frac{7}{8}$	$\frac{5}{16}$	$\frac{5}{16}$	1	1	$\frac{25}{32}$	1
6	50	$2\frac{5}{8}$	$\frac{1}{2}$	$\frac{1}{2}$	12	12	$19\frac{3}{8}$	$19\frac{1}{8}$	$18\frac{1}{2}$	18	$\frac{5}{16}$	$\frac{5}{16}$	1	1	$\frac{3}{4}$	$1\frac{1}{2}$
7	41	$2\frac{1}{2}$	$\frac{7}{16}$	$\frac{7}{16}$	10	$9\frac{7}{8}$	18	$17\frac{3}{4}$	17	$16\frac{5}{8}$	$\frac{21}{64}$	$\frac{21}{64}$	$1\frac{1}{64}$	$1\frac{1}{64}$	$\frac{23}{32}$	2
8	33	$2\frac{3}{8}$	$\frac{3}{8}$	$\frac{3}{8}$	8	$7\frac{7}{8}$	17	$16\frac{3}{4}$	$15\frac{1}{2}$	$15\frac{1}{4}$	$\frac{11}{32}$	$\frac{11}{32}$	$1\frac{1}{32}$	$1\frac{1}{32}$	$\frac{11}{16}$	$2\frac{5}{8}$

Table of link motion, cylinder 16 inches diameter; stroke 24 inches; steam-ports 15x1¼ inches; exhaust-ports 15x2½ inches; throw of eccentric 5½ inches; lead ⅛ inch full stroke, centre of stud on saddle 1 inch back of centre line of link, toward axle; outside lap ¾ inch on each end of valve; face of valve being 1½ inches longer than the total distance between outside edges of steam ports; inside lap 1-16 inch on each end of valve; the cavity or throat of valve being ⅛ inch narrower than the distance between inner edges of steam-ports, rocker-shaft being used.

VALVE TABLE OF LINK MOTION—NO. XV.

Notches.	Per cent. of admission.	Travel of valve.	Opening of Steam Port		Steam Cuts off. Expansion begins,		Exhaust Opens.		Exhaust closes, and Compression begins		Lead on Steam Port		Lead on Exhaust.		Slip of Link.	Lead commences from end of stroke
			Front Stroke	Back Stroke	Front Stroke	Back Stroke	Front Stroke	Back Stroke	Front Stroke	Back Stroke	Front Stroke	Back Stroke	Front Stroke	Back Stroke		
		Inch.	Inch.	Inch.	Inch.	Inch.	Inch.	Inch.	Inch.	Inch.	Inch.	Inch.	Inch.	Inch.	Inch.	Inch.
1	90	$5\frac{1}{2}$	$1\frac{15}{16}$	$2\frac{3}{32}$	$21\frac{5}{8}$	$21\frac{3}{4}$	$23\frac{3}{8}$	$23\frac{3}{8}$	$23\frac{1}{4}$	$23\frac{1}{4}$	$\frac{1}{8}$	$\frac{1}{8}$	$\frac{13}{16}$	$\frac{13}{16}$	$1\frac{1}{8}$	0
2	79	$3\frac{7}{8}$	$1\frac{1}{8}$	$1\frac{1}{4}$	19	$19\frac{1}{16}$	$22\frac{3}{8}$	$22\frac{7}{16}$	$21\frac{7}{8}$	$21\frac{7}{8}$	$\frac{1}{4}$	$\frac{1}{4}$	$\frac{15}{16}$	$\frac{15}{16}$	$1\frac{1}{16}$	$\frac{1}{8}$
3	71	$3\frac{5}{16}$	$\frac{7}{8}$	$\frac{15}{16}$	17	17	$21\frac{1}{2}$	$21\frac{1}{2}$	$20\frac{3}{4}$	$20\frac{3}{4}$	$\frac{5}{16}$	$\frac{5}{16}$	1	1	$\frac{1}{2}$	$\frac{3}{8}$
4	62	3	$\frac{3}{4}$	$\frac{3}{4}$	15	15	$20\frac{5}{8}$	$20\frac{5}{8}$	$19\frac{7}{8}$	$19\frac{7}{8}$	$\frac{11}{32}$	$\frac{11}{32}$	$1\frac{1}{32}$	$1\frac{1}{32}$	$\frac{7}{16}$	$\frac{9}{16}$
5	59	$2\frac{3}{4}$	$\frac{5}{8}$	$\frac{5}{8}$	$13\frac{1}{2}$	$13\frac{1}{2}$	$19\frac{3}{4}$	$19\frac{3}{4}$	$19\frac{1}{16}$	19	$\frac{11}{32}$	$\frac{11}{32}$	$1\frac{1}{32}$	$1\frac{1}{32}$	$\frac{3}{8}$	$\frac{3}{4}$
6	50	$2\frac{5}{8}$	$\frac{9}{16}$	$\frac{9}{16}$	12	12	$19\frac{1}{8}$	$19\frac{1}{8}$	18	18	$\frac{11}{32}$	$\frac{11}{32}$	$1\frac{1}{32}$	$1\frac{1}{32}$	$\frac{11}{32}$	1
7	41	$2\frac{9}{16}$	$\frac{1}{2}$	$\frac{1}{2}$	10	10	18	18	$16\frac{3}{4}$	$16\frac{7}{8}$	$\frac{23}{64}$	$\frac{23}{64}$	$1\frac{3}{64}$	$1\frac{3}{64}$	$\frac{5}{16}$	$1\frac{3}{8}$
8	33	$2\frac{13}{32}$	$\frac{7}{16}$	$\frac{7}{16}$	8	8	$16\frac{3}{4}$	$16\frac{5}{8}$	$15\frac{3}{8}$	$15\frac{1}{4}$	$\frac{23}{64}$	$\frac{23}{64}$	$1\frac{3}{64}$	$1\frac{3}{64}$	$\frac{9}{32}$	$1\frac{3}{4}$

Table of Link Motion, cylinder 16 inches diameter; stroke 24 inches; steam-ports 15x 1¼ inches; exhaust ports, 15 x 2½ inches; throw of eccentric 5½ inches; lead 1-8 inch, in full stroke; centre of stud on saddle ¼ inch back of centre line of link, toward axle; outside lap ¾ inch on each end of valve, inside lap 1-16 inch on each end of valve, throat of valve being ⅛ inch narrower than the distance between inner edges of steam-ports; rocker-shaft being used.

TABLE No. 16.—Shows the effect of changing the location of lifting-shaft, by removing it from above the centre of axle and placing it on the same vertical line of engine, below centre ot axle. It will be understood that tables No's 15 and 16 were taken from the same engine, no other alteration being made whatever, except the changing of position of lifting-shaft, which was 12½ inches above centre line ot axle, it being changed to 15½ inches below centre line of axle, that being the proper location when placed below the centre line of axle, the cylinder being elevated $\frac{5}{32}$ inch to the foot. By referring to the tables, we learn that there is no particular gain produced by the changing of the location of lifting-shaft in the distribution of steam, as admission, expansion, compression and release take place at the same time in both tables.

TABLE No. 15.—Shows a slight gain in the opening of steam-ports, for the first and second notches, that being of no importance, as no gain would be derived from the increase ot opening for these two notches, the full-stroke notches having sufficient opening to supply the demand for the cylinder ; the notches at and approaching mid-gear, is where an increase of opening would be of importance, as the steam be comes wire-drawn by the small opening of steam-port, which cannot be avoided when using the link as a cut-off.

TABLES No.'s 8 and 18.—Showing the effect of lap, both engines having the same motion, except the out-

VALVE TABLE OF LINK MOTION—NO. XVI.

Notches.	Per cent. of admission.	Travel of valve.	Opening of Steam Port		Steam cuts off, Expansion begins.		Exhaust Opens.		Exhaust closes, and compression begins.		Lead on Steam Port		Lead on Exhaust.		Slip of Link.	Lead commences from end of stroke
			Front Stroke	Back Stroke	Front Stroke	Back Stroke	Front Stroke	Back Stroke	Front Stroke	Back Stroke	Front Stroke	Back Stroke	Front Stroke	Back Stroke		
		Inch.	Inch.	Inch.	Inch.	Inch.	Inch.	Inch.	Inch.	Inch.	Inch.	Inch.	Inch.	Inch.	Inch.	Inch.
1	91	5 1/2	2	1 13/16	21 3/4	22	23 1/2	23 9/16	23 3/4	23 5/16	1/8	1/8	13/16	13/16	1	0
2	79	3 7/8	1 1/4	1 1/8	19	19 1/8	22 3/8	22 7/16	21 7/8	22	1/4	1/4	15/16	15/16	1/2	3/16
3	71	3 5/16	15/16	29/32	17	17	21 1/2	21 1/2	20 7/8	20 7/8	5/16	5/16	1	1	3/8	5/16
4	62	3	25/32	3/4	15	15	20 1/2	20 1/2	20	20	11/32	11/32	1	1	5/16	3/8
5	59	2 7/8	21/32	21/32	13 1/2	13 1/2	19 3/4	19 3/4	19	19	11/32	11/32	1 1/32	1 1/32	1/4	7/8
6	50	2 21/32	5/8	5/8	12	12	18 7/8	19	18	18	3/8	3/8	1 1/16	1 1/16	1/4	1 1/16
7	41	2 1/2	1/2	1/2	10	10	18	18	16 7/8	16 7/8	3/8	3/8	1 1/16	1 1/16	1/4	1 3/8
8	33	2 3/8	15/32	15/32	8	8	16 1/4	16 1/8	15 1/4	15 1/4	3/8	3/8	1 1/16	1 1/16	7/32	1 7/8

Table of link motion, cylinder 16x24 inches; steam-ports 15x1 1/4 inches; exhaust-port 15x2 1/2 inches; throw of eccentric 5 1/2 inches; lead 1/8 inch, in full stroke; centre of stud on saddle 1/4 inch back of centre line of link, toward axle; outside lap 3/4 inch on each end of valve, inside lap 1-16 inch on each end of valve; throat of valve being 1/8 inch narrower than the distance between inner edges of steam-ports, rocker-shaft used.

VALVE TABLE OF LINK MOTION.—NO. XVII.

Notches.	Per cent of admission.	Travel of valve.	Steam cuts off. Expansion begins.		Opening of Steam Port		Exhaust Opens.		Exhaust closes, and compression begins.		Lead on Steam Port		Lead on Exhaust.		Slip of link.	Lead commences from end of stroke
			Front Stroke	Back Stroke	Front Stroke	Back Stroke	Front Stroke	Back Stroke	Front Stroke	Back Stroke	Front Stroke	Back Stroke	Front Stroke	Back Stroke		
		Inch.	Inch.	Inch.	Inch.	Inch.	Inch.	Inch.	Inch.	Inch.	Inch.	Inch.	Inch.	Inch.	Inch.	Inch,
1	90	5	21½	21¾	1¾	1⅝	23¼	23½	23 1/16	23 3/16	1/16	1/16	11/16	11/16	11/16	0
2	79	3⅞	19	19¼	1¼	1⅛	22⅞	23	22 3/16	22¼	5/32	5/32	25/32	25/32	½	1/16
3	71	3⅛	17	17⅛	⅞	13/16	22	22 1/16	20¾	20¾	3/16	3/16	13/16	13/16	⅜	⅛
4	62	2⅞	15	15	11/16	11/16	21¼	21¼	19⅝	19⅝	¼	¼	⅞	⅞	5/16	¼
5	59	2⅝	13½	13½	9/16	9/16	20¾	20¾	18¾	18¾	¼	¼	⅞	⅞	¼	⅜
6	50	2 7/16	12	12	½	½	19¾	19¾	17⅞	17⅞	¼	¼	⅞	⅞	3/16	⅝
7	41	2⅜	10	10	7/16	7/16	19	19	16⅞	16⅜	17/64	17/64	57/64	57/64	9/64	⅞
8	33	2¼	8	7⅞	⅜	⅜	18	17⅞	15⅜	15⅛	9/32	9/32	29/32	29/32	⅛	1¼

Table of link motion, cylinder 16 inches diameter; stroke 24 inches; steam-ports 14x1¼ inches; exhaust-ports 14x2½ inches; throw of eccentric 5 inches; lead 1-16 inch full stroke, centre of stud on saddle ⅛ inch back of centre line of link, toward axle; outside lap ¾ inch on each end of valve; face of valve being 1½ inches longer than the extreme distance between outside edges of steam ports; inside lap ⅛ inch on each end of valve; the cavity or throat of valve being ¼ inch narrower than the distance between inner edges of steam-ports, rocker-shaft being used.

side lap. Table No. 18, cylinder 16 inches in diameter; stroke 24 inches; throw of eccentric 5 inches; lap ¾ inch on each end of valve, face of valve being 1½ inches longer than the total distance between the outside edges of steam-ports, inside having no lap; throat or cavity of valve being the same width as the distance between the inner edges of steam-ports.

TABLE No. 18.—With ¾ inch outside lap, shows that the steam follows the piston 8 per cent. further, when working in full-stroke notch, than is shown in table No. 8, with 1 inch outside lap. For all the rest of the notches we find a gain much in favor of Table No. 8, with 1 inch outside lap, above Table No. 18, with ¾ inch outside lap, as the steam is deferred to 3 per cent. later period of the stroke. We also find, by referring to Table No. 8, with 1 inch outside lap, that compression takes place 8 per cent. later in the stroke, on an average, for all the notches, from the fifth to the eighth notch, above that shown in Valve Table No. 18, with ¾ inch lap. We also find that premature lead is reduced to a proper quantity, by increasing the lap to 1 inch outside. By referring to Table No. 8, we find 40 per cent. less premature lead than is shown in Table No. 18. By referring back to Table No. 7, with 1 inch outside lap, and ¼ inch inside lap, we have decreased the power of engine, as the table shows that, by adding inside lap, we increase compression 14 per cent., while expansion is only increased 9 per cent., and does not show as good a working table as Table No. 18, with ¾ inch outside, and no inside lap.

10

VALVE TABLE OF LINK MOTION—NO. XVIII.

Notches.	Per cent. of admission.	Travel of valve.	Opening of Steam Port		Steam cuts off, Expansion begins.		Exhaust Opens.		Exhaust closes, and compression begins.		Lead on Steam Port		Lead on Exhaust.		Slip of Link.	Lead commences from end of stroke
			Front Stroke	Back Stroke	Front Stroke	Back Stroke	Front Stroke	Back Stroke	Front Stroke	Back Stroke	Front Stroke	Back Stroke	Front Stroke	Back Stroke		
		Inch.	Inch.	Inch.	Inch.	Inch.	Inch.	Inch.	Inch.	Inch.	Inch.	Inch.	Inch.	Inch.	Inch.	Inch.
1	90	$4\frac{15}{16}$	$1\frac{3}{4}$	$1\frac{5}{8}$	$21\frac{1}{2}$	$21\frac{3}{4}$	$23\frac{1}{16}$	$23\frac{5}{16}$	$23\frac{1}{16}$	$23\frac{5}{16}$	$\frac{1}{16}$	$\frac{1}{16}$	$\frac{13}{16}$	$\frac{13}{16}$	$\frac{11}{16}$	0
2	79	$3\frac{7}{8}$	$1\frac{1}{4}$	$1\frac{1}{8}$	19	$19\frac{1}{4}$	$22\frac{1}{2}$	$22\frac{9}{16}$	$22\frac{1}{2}$	$22\frac{9}{16}$	$\frac{5}{32}$	$\frac{5}{32}$	$\frac{29}{32}$	$\frac{29}{32}$	$\frac{1}{2}$	$\frac{1}{16}$
3	71	$3\frac{1}{8}$	$\frac{7}{8}$	$\frac{13}{16}$	17	$17\frac{1}{8}$	$21\frac{1}{2}$	$21\frac{1}{2}$	$21\frac{1}{2}$	$21\frac{1}{2}$	$\frac{7}{32}$	$\frac{7}{32}$	$\frac{31}{32}$	$\frac{31}{32}$	$\frac{3}{8}$	$\frac{1}{8}$
4	62	$2\frac{7}{8}$	$\frac{11}{16}$	$\frac{11}{16}$	15	15	$20\frac{1}{2}$	$20\frac{1}{2}$	$20\frac{1}{2}$	$20\frac{1}{2}$	$\frac{1}{4}$	$\frac{1}{4}$	1	1	$\frac{5}{16}$	$\frac{1}{4}$
5	59	$2\frac{5}{8}$	$\frac{9}{16}$	$\frac{9}{16}$	$13\frac{1}{2}$	$13\frac{1}{2}$	$19\frac{3}{4}$	$19\frac{3}{4}$	$19\frac{3}{4}$	$19\frac{3}{4}$	$\frac{1}{4}$	$\frac{1}{4}$	1	1	$\frac{1}{4}$	$\frac{3}{8}$
6	50	$2\frac{7}{16}$	$\frac{1}{2}$	$\frac{1}{2}$	12	12	19	19	19	19	$\frac{1}{4}$	$\frac{1}{4}$	1	1	$\frac{3}{16}$	$\frac{5}{8}$
7	41	$2\frac{3}{8}$	$\frac{7}{16}$	$\frac{7}{16}$	10	10	18	$17\frac{7}{8}$	18	$17\frac{7}{8}$	$\frac{17}{64}$	$\frac{17}{64}$	$1\frac{1}{64}$	$1\frac{1}{64}$	$\frac{9}{64}$	$\frac{7}{8}$
8	33	$2\frac{1}{4}$	$\frac{3}{8}$	$\frac{3}{8}$	8	8	$16\frac{3}{4}$	$16\frac{5}{8}$	$16\frac{3}{4}$	$16\frac{5}{8}$	$\frac{9}{32}$	$\frac{9}{32}$	$1\frac{1}{32}$	$1\frac{1}{32}$	$\frac{1}{8}$	$1\frac{1}{4}$

Table of link motion, cylinder 17 inches diameter; stroke 24 inches; steam-ports 16x1¼ inches; exhaust-port 16x2½ inches; throw of eccentric 5 inches; lead 1-16 inch, in full stroke; centre of stud on saddle ⅛ inch back of centre line of link, toward axle; outside lap ¾ inch on each end of valve; face of valve 1½ inches longer than the extreme distance between outside edges of steam-ports; inside no lap; width of cavity or throat of valve the total distance between inner edges of steam-port; rocker-shaft used.

VALVE TABLE OF LINK MOTION—NO. XIX.

Notches.	Per cent. of admission.	Travel of valve.	Opening of Steam Port		Steam Cuts off. Expansion begins,		Exhaust Opens.		Exhaust closes, and Compression begins.		Lead on Steam Port		Lead on Exhaust.		Slip of Link.	Lead commences from end of stroke
			Front Stroke	Back Stroke	Front Stroke	Back Stroke	Front Stroke	Back Stroke	Front Stroke	Back Stroke	Front Stroke	Back Stroke	Front Stroke	Back Stroke		
		Inch.	Inch.	Inch.	Inch.	Inch.	Inch.	Inch.	Inch.	Inch.	Inch.	Inch.	Inch.	Inch.	Inch.	Inch.
1	88	$4\frac{1}{2}$	$1\frac{5}{8}$	$1\frac{1}{2}$	$19\frac{3}{8}$	$19\frac{5}{8}$	$21\frac{3}{8}$	$21\frac{3}{8}$	$21\frac{1}{4}$	$21\frac{1}{4}$	$\frac{1}{16}$	$\frac{1}{16}$	$\frac{3}{4}$	$\frac{3}{4}$	$\frac{3}{4}$	0
2	82	$3\frac{7}{8}$	$1\frac{1}{4}$	$1\frac{3}{16}$	18	$18\frac{3}{8}$	21	$21\frac{1}{8}$	$20\frac{1}{2}$	$20\frac{5}{8}$	$\frac{1}{8}$	$\frac{1}{8}$	$\frac{13}{16}$	$\frac{13}{16}$	$\frac{5}{8}$	0
3	73	$3\frac{1}{4}$	$\frac{7}{8}$	$\frac{7}{8}$	16	$16\frac{1}{4}$	$20\frac{1}{8}$	$20\frac{3}{8}$	$19\frac{5}{8}$	$19\frac{3}{4}$	$\frac{3}{16}$	$\frac{3}{16}$	$\frac{7}{8}$	$\frac{7}{8}$	$\frac{7}{16}$	$\frac{1}{8}$
4	63	$2\frac{11}{16}$	$\frac{5}{8}$	$\frac{5}{8}$	14	$14\frac{1}{8}$	$19\frac{1}{8}$	$19\frac{1}{8}$	$18\frac{1}{2}$	$18\frac{1}{2}$	$\frac{7}{32}$	$\frac{7}{32}$	$\frac{29}{32}$	$\frac{29}{32}$	$\frac{5}{16}$	$\frac{1}{4}$
5	56	$2\frac{1}{2}$	$\frac{9}{16}$	$\frac{9}{16}$	$12\frac{1}{2}$	$12\frac{1}{2}$	$18\frac{3}{4}$	$18\frac{3}{4}$	$17\frac{3}{4}$	$17\frac{3}{4}$	$\frac{1}{4}$	$\frac{1}{4}$	$\frac{15}{16}$	$\frac{15}{16}$	$\frac{1}{4}$	$\frac{5}{16}$
6	50	$2\frac{3}{8}$	$\frac{1}{2}$	$\frac{1}{2}$	11	11	18	18	17	17	$\frac{1}{4}$	$\frac{1}{4}$	$\frac{15}{16}$	$\frac{15}{16}$	$\frac{3}{16}$	$\frac{3}{8}$
7	41	$2\frac{1}{4}$	$\frac{3}{8}$	$\frac{3}{8}$	9	9	$17\frac{1}{8}$	$17\frac{1}{8}$	16	16	$\frac{1}{4}$	$\frac{1}{4}$	$\frac{15}{16}$	$\frac{15}{16}$	$\frac{5}{32}$	$\frac{5}{8}$
8	32	$2\frac{1}{8}$	$\frac{11}{32}$	$\frac{11}{32}$	7	$6\frac{7}{8}$	$15\frac{3}{4}$	$15\frac{3}{8}$	$14\frac{5}{8}$	$14\frac{5}{8}$	$\frac{17}{64}$	$\frac{17}{64}$	$\frac{61}{64}$	$\frac{61}{64}$	$\frac{1}{8}$	1

Table of Link Motion, cylinder 16 inches diameter; stroke 22 inches; steam-ports 14x 1¼ inches; exhaust ports, 14 x 2½ inches; throw of eccentric 4½ inches; lead 1-16 inch, in full stroke; centre of stud on saddle ⅛ inch back of centre line of link, toward axle; outside lap ¾ inch on each end of valve, face of valve being 1½ inches longer than the total distance between the outside edges of steam-ports; inside lap 1-16 inch on each end of valve; cavity or throat of valve being ⅛ inch narrower than the distance between inner edges of steam-ports; rocker-shaft being used.

We learn, from the tables, that lap may be increased to such extent as to work the steam about one-third, or a trifle over, of the stroke, expansively, when cutting off the steam at one-third of the stroke, leaving nearly one-third for compression. By increasing the inside lap, to work the steam by expansion, to a later period, the compression will take place earlier in the stroke, to the same amount as expansion is deferred, the compression creating a greater resistance than is gained by the increased period of expansion of steam, as the pressure of steam is reduced and compression increased. By cutting off at an earlier period than one-third of stroke the steam becomes too much wire-drawn, as the opening of steam-port will not be sufficient to fill the demand of cylinder. To accomplish much work a valve may be made to cut off at one-tenth of the stroke, when using two valves, one as a cut-off valve, the other as a main valve, the same as the old fashioned hook motion, with independent cut-off.

We learn from the valve tables given, that the distribution of steam is not affected by changing the width of steam-ports, by cutting them out, or narrowing up the bridges between the steam and exhaust ports, if the valve be changed also, so as to have the same lap and lead as before the ports were widened; as we learn from the tables that lap, lead, and travel of valve control the distribution of steam, the valve controlling the four distinct movements of steam for each revolution of the crank: admission, expansion,

VALVE TABLE OF LINK MOTION.—NO. XX.

Notches.	Per cent. of admission.	Travel of valve.	Opening of Steam Port		Steam cuts off. Expansion begins.		Exhaust Opens.		Exhaust closes, and compression begins.		Lead on Steam Port		Lead on Exhaust.		Slip of link.	Lead commences from end of stroke
			Front Stroke	Back Stroke	Front Stroke	Back Stroke	Front Stroke	Back Stroke	Front Stroke	Back Stroke	Front Stroke	Back Stroke	Front Stroke	Back Stroke		
		Inch.	Inch.	Inch.	Inch.	Inch.	Inch.	Inch.	Inch.	Inch.	Inch.	Inch.	Inch.	Inch.	Inch.	Inch,
1	90	$4\frac{15}{16}$	$1\frac{3}{4}$	$1\frac{5}{8}$	$21\frac{1}{2}$	$21\frac{3}{4}$	$23\frac{9}{16}$	$23\frac{11}{16}$	$22\frac{7}{8}$	$22\frac{3}{4}$	$\frac{1}{16}$	$\frac{1}{16}$	$\frac{9}{16}$	$\frac{9}{16}$	$\frac{11}{16}$	0
2	79	$3\frac{7}{8}$	$1\frac{1}{4}$	$1\frac{1}{8}$	19	$19\frac{1}{4}$	$23\frac{1}{4}$	$23\frac{5}{16}$	$21\frac{3}{4}$	$21\frac{7}{8}$	$\frac{5}{32}$	$\frac{5}{32}$	$\frac{21}{32}$	$\frac{21}{32}$	$\frac{1}{2}$	$\frac{1}{16}$
3	71	$3\frac{1}{8}$	$\frac{7}{8}$	$\frac{13}{16}$	17	$17\frac{1}{8}$	$22\frac{1}{2}$	$22\frac{1}{2}$	$20\frac{1}{8}$	$20\frac{1}{8}$	$\frac{3}{16}$	$\frac{3}{16}$	$\frac{11}{16}$	$\frac{11}{16}$	$\frac{3}{8}$	$\frac{1}{8}$
4	62	$2\frac{7}{8}$	$\frac{11}{16}$	$\frac{11}{16}$	15	15	22	$21\frac{7}{8}$	19	$18\frac{7}{8}$	$\frac{1}{4}$	$\frac{1}{4}$	$\frac{3}{4}$	$\frac{3}{4}$	$\frac{5}{16}$	$\frac{1}{4}$
5	59	$2\frac{5}{8}$	$\frac{9}{16}$	$\frac{9}{16}$	$13\frac{1}{2}$	$13\frac{1}{2}$	$21\frac{3}{8}$	$21\frac{3}{8}$	18	$17\frac{15}{16}$	$\frac{1}{4}$	$\frac{1}{4}$	$\frac{3}{4}$	$\frac{3}{4}$	$\frac{1}{4}$	$\frac{3}{8}$
6	50	$2\frac{7}{16}$	$\frac{1}{2}$	$\frac{1}{2}$	12	12	$20\frac{3}{4}$	$20\frac{3}{4}$	$16\frac{3}{4}$	$16\frac{3}{4}$	$\frac{9}{64}$	$\frac{9}{64}$	$\frac{49}{64}$	$\frac{49}{64}$	$\frac{3}{16}$	$\frac{5}{8}$
7	41	$2\frac{3}{8}$	$\frac{7}{16}$	$\frac{7}{16}$	10	10	20	$19\frac{3}{4}$	$15\frac{3}{4}$	$15\frac{1}{2}$	$\frac{9}{64}$	$\frac{9}{64}$	$\frac{25}{32}$	$\frac{25}{32}$	$\frac{5}{32}$	$\frac{7}{8}$
8	33	$2\frac{1}{4}$	$\frac{3}{8}$	$\frac{3}{8}$	8	8	19	$18\frac{3}{4}$	$14\frac{1}{8}$	$13\frac{7}{8}$	$\frac{9}{64}$	$\frac{9}{64}$	$\frac{25}{32}$	$\frac{25}{32}$	$\frac{1}{8}$	$1\frac{1}{4}$

Table of link motion, cylinder 16 inches diameter; stroke 24 inches; steam-ports 15x1¼ inches; exhaust-port 15x2½ inches; throw of eccentric 5 inches; lead 1-16 inch full stroke, centre of stud on saddle ⅛ inch back of centre line of link, toward axle; outside lap ¾ inch on each end of valve; face of valve being 1½ inches longer than the extreme distance between outside edges of steam ports; inside lap ¼ inch on each end of valve; the cavity or throat of valve being ½ inch narrower than the distance between inner edges of steam-ports, rocker-shaft being used.

VALVE TABLE OF LINK MOTION—NO. XXI.

Notches.	Per cent. of admission.	Travel of valve.	Opening of Steam Port		Steam cuts off, Expansion begins.		Exhaust Opens.		Exhaust closes, and compression begins.		Lead on Steam Port		Lead on Exhaust.		Slip of Link	Lead commences from end of stroke
			Front Stroke	Back Stroke	Front Stroke	Back Stroke	Front Stroke	Back Stroke	Front Stroke	Back Stroke	Front Stroke	Back Stroke	Front Stroke	Back Stroke		
		Inch.	Inch.	Inch.	Inch.	Inch.	Inch.	Inch.	Inch.	Inch.	Inch.	Inch.	Inch.	Inch.	Inch.	Inch.
1	90	5	2 1/16	1 7/8	21 1/2	21 5/8	23 1/4	23 3/8	23 1/16	23 1/8	1/8	1/8	13/16	13/16	1 1/8	0
2	79	4	1 5/16	1 3/32	19 1/16	19 1/16	22 1/4	22 1/4	21 7/8	21 7/8	5/16	5/16	1	1	5/8	1/16
3	71	3 7/16	1	31/32	17	17	21 3/8	21 3/8	20 7/8	20 7/8	3/8	3/8	1 1/16	1 1/16	3/8	3/8
4	62	3 1/16	13/16	13/16	15	15	20 1/2	20 1/2	19 3/4	19 3/4	3/8	3/8	1 1/16	1 1/16	5/16	5/8
5	59	2 7/8	11/16	11/16	13 1/2	13 1/2	19 3/4	19 3/4	18 3/4	18 3/4	13/32	11/32	1 3/32	1 3/32	9/32	7/8
6	50	2 11/16	5/8	5/8	12	12	18 7/8	18 7/8	17 7/8	17 7/8	13/32	11/32	1 3/32	1 3/32	1/4	1 3/16
7	41	2 9/16	1/2	1/2	10	10	17 3/4	17 3/4	16 1/2	16 1/2	13/32	11/32	1 3/32	1 3/32	5/32	1 5/8
8	33	2 7/16	7/16	7/16	8	8	16 1/8	16 1/8	15	15	13/32	11/32	1 3/32	1 3/32	1/8	2 1/4

Table of link motion, cylinder 18 inches diameter; stroke 24 inches; steam-ports 17x1¼ inches; exhaust-port 17x2½ inches; throw of eccentric 5 inches; lead 1-8 inch, in full stroke; centre of stud on saddle ⅛ inch back of centre line of link, toward axle; outside lap ¾ inch on each end of valve; face of valve 1½ inches longer than the extreme distance between outside edges of steam-ports; inside lap 1-16 inch on each end of valve; throat or cavity of valve being ½ inch narrower than the distance between inside edges of steam-ports; rocker-shaft used.

compression and exhaust. The outside edges of steam-ports, with outside edges of valve, regulate the admission and expansion, while the inner edges of the steam-port, with inner edges of valve, regulate the exhaust and compression; as lap, lead, and travel of valve regulate the distribution of steam, and alteration of any of these will affect the motion in a definable manner. As the period of admission varies with the variation of either lap, lead, or travel of valve, so also does that of expansion, which increases as the admission decreases; and a reduction of the period of admission will be the result of an increase of lap or increase of lead, or reduction of travel of valve. Each of these elements reach their extreme qualities, as shown by the tables, as follows: lap 1 inch on each end of valve, for fast time, inside, line-and-line; for freight $\frac{3}{4}$ inch on each end of valve, inside, line-and-line; lead not to exceed $\frac{1}{16}$ inch in full stroke; when required to work engine in the mid-gear notches travel of valve reaches its maximum when traveling the distance equal to the width of both steam-ports and lap of both ends of valve, added together; to the quotient, add $\frac{1}{2}$ inch, this will give the maximum of travel of valve.

These tables answer for all engines, whether 20, 22, or 24-inch stroke, as we learn from the tables that the point of suspension would be the only point affected by the changing of crank, from a 20-inch stroke to a 24-inch stroke engine, the eccentrics require the same position; also the same lengths of eccentric-rod for all lengths of stroke, when using the same valve motion.

The general influences common to the link motion has been pointed out and illustrated with tables with some minuteness, sufficient to show that a correct working link motion can be obtained for all cases. There is also a sufficient number of valve tables given, with different dimensions of lap, leads, and travel of valve, so that the engineer can find a table corresponding with the motion of his engine; also a table that will correspond with any alterations that he may suggest, giving a clear idea of his suggestions, without experimenting with his engine or the use of a model

MOVEMENT OF VALVE.

Notches.	Steam cuts off.		Opening of Steam Port		Valve stops traveling, Piston moves on.		Valve commences to move back again.		Distance Piston travels while valve has no motion.		Travel of valve.
	Front Stroke	Back Stroke	Front Stroke	Back Stroke	Front Stroke	Back Stroke	Front Stroke	Back Stroke	Front Stroke	Back Stroke	
	Inch.	Inch.	Inch.	Inch.	Inch.	Inch.	Inch.	Inch.	Inch.	Inch.	Inch.
1	20¼	20¾	1 13/16	1 11/16	7¼	8	9½	11¼	2¼	3¼	5
2	19	19¼	1¼	1 3/16	5	5¼	8½	9¾	3½	4½	4 1/16
3	17	17⅛	⅞	⅞	4½	4¾	7¼	8¼	2¾	3¾	3½
4	15	15	¾	¾	3⅜	3½	5¾	6½	2⅜	3	3⅛
5	13½	13½	⅝	⅝	2½	2⅝	4½	5¼	2	2⅝	2 15/16
6	12	12	½	½	1⅞	2	4⅛	4¼	2⅛	2¼	2¾
7	10	10	13/32	13/32	1½	1½	3	3⅛	1½	1⅝	2⅝
8	8	8	11/32	11/32	¾	¾	2	2	1¼	1¼	2⅜

This table shows the distance the Piston moves from the commencement of its stroke; before the Valve gives its full travel or opening of steam port, when there is no loss motion. Also, showing the distance that the Piston travels while the valve has no movement, for a short period after reaching its full travel before commencing to move back again. This table was taken from Engine Cylinder 16x24 inches; link motion; rocker-shaft used. Throw of eccentric, 5 inches; outside lap of valve, ⅞ inch on each end; inside lap, 1-16 inch on each end; lead on steam port, 1-16 inch full stroke.

TABLE OF LAP AND LEAD.

Showing the amount of lap, lead, and travel of valve, used in Locomotive Engines now running in the United States:

Locomotives running in the vicinity of New York City, N. Y.

FAST EXPRESS TRAINS.

	Inches.
Outside lap, from	$\frac{3}{4}$ to $\frac{7}{8}$
Inside lap, (mostly line-and-line) to	$\frac{1}{16}$
Lead, full stroke	$\frac{1}{16}$
Throw of eccentric	$4\frac{1}{2}$ to $5\frac{1}{4}$

FREIGHT ENGINES.

Outside lap, from	$\frac{11}{16}$ to $\frac{3}{4}$
Inside lap, (mostly line-and-line) to	$\frac{1}{16}$
Lead, full stroke, from	$\frac{1}{16}$ to $\frac{1}{10}$
Throw of eccentric, from	$4\frac{1}{2}$ to 5

Vicinity of Boston.

FAST EXPRESS TRAINS.

Outside lap, from	$\frac{3}{4}$ to 1
Inside lap, (line-and-line)	
Lead, full stroke, from	$\frac{1}{32}$ to $\frac{1}{16}$
Throw of eccentric, from	$4\frac{3}{4}$ to $5\frac{1}{4}$

Buffalo, Cincinnati, St. Louis, New Orleans, and Western Roads.

Outside lap, from	$\frac{5}{8}$ to $\frac{7}{8}$
Inside lap, (line-and-line) to	$\frac{1}{8}$
Travel of valve, from	$4\frac{1}{2}$ to 5
Lead, full stroke, from	$\frac{1}{32}$ to $\frac{1}{10}$

MANAGEMENT OF LOCOMOTIVE.

Duty of an Engineer, and Management of an Engine.

The duty of an engineer is to know when his engine is in good order, so as to be ready for duty when required.

It is also the duty of an engineer to thoroughly understand the time card, and rules and regulations of the road that he is employed on, so that he may know his rights of the road, and avoid all mistakes.

When running by orders he must not leave a station until he is positive that he understands the order given.

When on the road he should keep a diligent watch, to see that the road is clear, and a good lookout for signals, so that he can stop his train in time, if possible.

An engine must be handled with care, and should work its steam expansively, by cutting off the steam as closely as possible, which is done by the reverse lever, after the engine has gained its headway. There is a large amount of fuel saved by working the steam expansively. In this particular point a great difference is shown in fuel, also in the wear of an engine, when different engineers run the same engine for some length of time.

In firing an engine a little good judgment is very requisite, as it gets steam and saves fuel. It is also necessary to study the nature of the fuel, to know how to fire it.

When burning wood the furnace door must be kept open as short a time as possible ; if the draught-pipe is of proper size, and located right, with proper proportioned stack, there will be no need of filling up the furnace above the door with wood. Care should be taken not to throw the wood against the flue ends, as it will cause them to leak. Keep the damper open in firing, when using steam. Every engine should have two dampers, one on each end of ash pan, to avoid trouble in snow storms ; the dampers and door should never be closed at the same time, when working steam, as it will cause the flues to leak. The fire should be very low on reaching terminal station. On approaching a heavy grade the engine should be properly primed with a good head of steam and a furnace full of wood, and kept so while ascending the grade. The dampers should be perfectly tight, so when shut, and not using steam, there will be no steam generated. An engine, when blowing off steam, wastes fuel and water.

Anthracite coal requires an even heavy fire at all times. There is no necessity for dumping fire, only when necessary to wash the boiler. By drawing the coal to the back end of furnace, leaving the grate-bars bare in front, the fire may be kept for a week, if necessary.

Bituminous coal is very different from anthracite, it comprising many different kinds and qualities, from a slack and slag mixed, to the pure block. The latter is almost equal to anthracite. Some of the former produces large quantities of clinker. As a general rule, a shallow fire is the best, and, by breaking the lumps into small pieces, will prevent it from clinkering, it there is not too much put in the furnace at one firing.

In carrying water in a Locomotive boiler it is best to carry the water as high as possible, and work dry steam, as the same heat will generate more steam from 900 gallons of water than it will from 800 gallons.

The valves and cylinders require to be oiled with melted tallow or lard oil. When running down grade it is well to have a little steam passing through the cylinders. Tallow should be used sparingly, and often; the valves and cylinders should be oiled always before going in the round house, to prevent them from rusting.

Damp steam or water should never be worked through the cylinders, if it can be avoided, as it does much harm, damaging the packing and roughening the valves and cylinders, and frequently cutting them; it also strains the engine, by compressing the water between the cylinder heads and piston.

The throttle should be pulled out just far enough to do the work required. An engine will run much easier with just enough steam, than it will with the full pressure of the boiler on the valves all the time.

Pumping properly is a very nice point in running an engine. An engineer should know that his pumps are all right, and be sure that they are working just as he wishes them. There is no honor in running 10 or

15 miles without trying the gauge-cocks to see where the water is. No engineer should put such confidence in his pumps, as they are very treacherous at times. An engineer should not run any further distance, without trying his water, than it would take his engine to use one gauge of water out of the boiler; then he would always be on the safe side. Burning an engine is generally caused by too mnch confidence being placed in pumps.

Examination should be made of the principal parts of the engine, such as the bearings, keys, nuts, and other parts of the running gear, as often as convenient, when stopping at stations along the road.

Care should be taken not to slip the tender truck wheels, by setting up the brakes too tight, as slipping heats and softens the chill, thus making flat spots on the wheels.

Use sand as little as possible, as it makes the train pull hard.

Care must be taken to avoid slipping the driving-wheels as much as possible, as it not only strains the engine but cuts out the tires.

An engineer should not start out on his run without a hammer and wrenches, such as are needed about his engine; also pinch-bar and jack-screws. The most important articles are a red light and red flag, particularly on roads having a single track.

No time should be lost in getting out a flag ahead of the engine, when, from any cause the train has to stand on main line, on approaching train's time.

Should the engine get off the rails the first duty is to notice the position in which the engine stands; if the front end pitches down, so as to take the water from the crown-sheet, or should the engine lie on its side, so as to take the water from the side sheet, then the fire must be put out. Either wood or coal fire can be put out by shoveling sand, sod, or ice into the furnace, if there is no water at hand.

If an engineer has an engine that does not steam free, the nozzles should not be made smaller, unless they are large sized for that class engine, in most cases, the exhaust nozzles are too small. The contracting of the exhaust nozzles should be the last resort to get steam. Contracting of nozzles, choking up top of stack, and increasing inside lap, all have the same effect in choking the engine.

The boiler should be kept clean by blowing out as often as the nature of the water may require; and, after blowing out, one of the gauge cocks or the blow-off cock should be kept open. If the blow-off cock and gauge cock are closed there will be a vacuum produced by the steam that is left in the boiler, and cause the flues to leak, if the boiler has been any length of time in use.

For loosening the scale in the boiler a little mahogany sawdust put in the boiler answers a very good purpose. The boiler should be blown out after the next trip.

A leaky boiler may be stopped by putting 2 pounds of common black tea in the boiler, some white oak bark, or some of the liquid from the bark. These articles will also prevent the water from foaming.

The eccentrics should be marked on the axle, so if they slip they can be easily set to their places again. If an eccentric should slip, and not be marked, it can be easily set by placing the full throw of the eccentric to the right angle position to the crank. This can be done by counting the spokes in the wheel; one-fourth of the number of spokes in the wheel, from the crank, will be the right angle position to the crank. The full throw of eccentric can now be set by the eye, to the right angle position to the crank, then mark the eccentric and axle to correspond with each other; if it is an indirect motion the rocker-shaft will be used, and the eccentrics must be moved toward the crank, from the mark made on the axle, 1½ times the distance of the lap and lead, when added together. For example: lap ¾ inch, lead ⅛ inch, total ⅞ inch; 1½ times ⅞ inch making 1 $\frac{5}{16}$ inch; 1 $\frac{5}{16}$ inch distance eccentric is to be moved toward crank, from mark made on axle. It will be understood that 1½ times the lap and lead will not define the position for all engines, but will answer for most of the engines now running on the roads in the United States. Some engines will require their eccentrics to be moved a trifle further than 1½ times the lap and lead; others a trifle less, as the diameter of axle and diameter and throw of eccentric, govern the the distance that the eccentric has to move around on the shaft, from the mark made. It will be understood, that the smaller the axle is, the less the distance to be moved. As a rule: by moving an eccentric 1½ times the lap and lead, as described above, will be near enough to its position for any engine to take its train to its destination. It will be so near right that it can be set just right, if necessary, by the exhaust; if a trifle too heavy, move the eccentric back a little from the crank; if the exhaust is a little too light, move the eccentric a trifle toward the crank. It is to be remembered, that when the rocker-shaft is used, the go-a-head, or forward eccentric, has to be moved forward, for lead, from the right angle position to the crank; and the back motion eccentric has to be moved backward, from the right angle position to the crank. The forward eccentric follows the crank when the engine is moving forward; the backing eccentric follows the crank when moving backward. When direct motion, no rocker shaft being used, the position of the eccentric will be right the reverse.

If any accident should occur to the connection of the valve-gear of one cylinder, when on the road, the main-rod and valve-rod must be disconnected on that side, and the piston moved to the back end of cylinder, and the valve moved back, so that there is a slight opening given to the front end of steam-port. This will hold the piston to the back end of cylinder; the back cylinder-cock should be taken out or left open; the front cock must be kept closed When this is done there is no occasion to block the cross-head.

In case of an eccentric-rod breaking, the eccentric-strap must be taken down; if it is left on it will turn around with the eccentric, and the extension, where the eccentric-rod fastens, will punch a hole in the leg of the boiler.

Should a branch-pipe burst, or the steam-chest get broken, the steam may be shut off from that side, so as to get in with one cylinder, by slackening up the nuts on the bolts of the top joint of branch-pipe, and slipping a piece of tank or thin iron between the end of branch-pipe and the brass ring; a piece cut out of the man-hole cover of the tank will do very nicely, if there is nothing else at hand.

The engine should not be reversed unless there is danger, as it strains the engine, and pumps hot air and cinders into the cylinders.

The packing should never be left in the stuffing-boxes until it is rotten and burned, as it then scratches the rods; nor should the packing be set up too tight, as it will make the engine work stiff, and pound, and may break the stuffing-box bolts.

In keying up the rods care must be taken not to get them too tight. When the parallel-rod boxes are fitted the engine must be placed on the centre, and stand on an even track, so that the boxes are the same height in both pedestals, The brasses at the back end of the rods must be left a little slack, so as to let the driving boxes rise and fall in the pedestals without straining the rods and keys.

If one parallel, or side rod, as it is called, should break, the one on the opposite side must be taken down; if left on it will break or twist the axle.

If a spring-strap break, and there is no extra strap on the engine, it can be held temporarily with a chain.

If a spring should break, when on the road, a piece of rubber and wood, or wood alone, must be put on top of the driving-box, to keep the box in its place.

If an engine should break down, when on the road, the engineer should make an effort to repair the parts broken, in such manner as to enable him to take his train to the next station or terminus of his run, as the circumstances may require.

When working with one cylinder, and the engine stops on the centre, with a heavy train, the engine and tender must be disconnected from the train, and the wheels slipped, so as to stand off the centre; with a light train it can be done with a pinch-bar.

If the throttle lever rod should break or become detached, let the steam down, so that the engine can be handled by the reverse lever. To stop, place the reverse lever so that the engine is in mid-gear, and apply the brakes. With the V hooks set the cut-off valve so as to cover its ports.

When an engine is foaming it can be detected by the spluttering sound of steam and water coming out of the gauge-cocks, when open, which is very different in sound from steam or water. If all the gauge-cocks give that spluttering sound, then it would be dangerous, in most cases, to shut off the steam to stop the engine, as the water would fall below the crown-sheet, and then the top flues and crown-sheet would become bare for want of water, and get red hot; the flues would collapse, and the crown-sheet would come down; there would be danger also of the boiler bursting. When an engine is foaming badly, the pump feed must be increased, and the engine throttled down a little, so as to lessen the speed until one or two gauge cocks show solid water. The pressure of steam must be kept up; if the steam is allowed to go down, then the water will fall with the steam and the engine will foam worse. The steam must be shut off carefully, to try the water, when within about a mile of the station, to see if there is sufficient water in the boiler to stop with safety, if not, the pump feed can be increased so as to get sufficient water by the time the station is reached. If, from any cause, sufficient water cannot be got into the boiler to stop with safety, and the train must be taken through, then, when approaching a station the engine must be cut loose from the train and be pumped up, which is termed running for water. If the boiler be filled full of water, and the engine run backward, the scum can be worked off through the cylinders; if there is no blow cock, then it will not go all over the engine; when this is done it will be of much benefit. The valves should always be oiled after working water through them. Engines foam from several causes: water containing alkali, lime, vegetable or animal matter will cause foaming, if the boiler is not washed out often. Oil, soap or soda, are the worst articles to produce foaming. New boilers will foam until the enamel is off the iron. Preventatives: wash boiler often; sugar, vinegar, tea, or white oak bark, will stop foaming.

It often occurs that when a locomotive engine has a pound, it is difficult for a young engineer to find the cause. To find the cause, an examination should be made of the connecting-rod brasses; if the brasses are not too loose on the pins the keys must not be driven to stop the pound, but proceed further to find the cause, by examining the driving-box brasses and driving-box wedges. Also, examine the set-screw that holds the back of the wedge against the pedestal, if it is too long it will press against the driving box, and cause a pound. Proceed next to caliper the tires to see if they are all the same size. If one tire is softer than the rest, that tire will wear faster than the rest, and become smaller in diameter, and will have to slip every revolution. The difference between the circumference of that tire and the larger ones, will cause a pound; or, if one tire is harder than the rest, so as not to wear as fast as the other tires, it will cause a pound, the same as if it was smaller. There will be no difficulty in finding the cause of the engine pounding, if proceeding as above described.

The cylinder-cocks may be used, when the valves or packing blows, to find out where the blow is located. When testing the valves, the reverse lever must be in the centre notch, so that the engine will be in mid-gear, and the crank-pin vertical with the centre of axle; or, in other words, the position of crank must be at half-stroke, on the side of engine to be examined. Next in order, set the tender brake, and admit steam in the steam-chest. Should the valve not be tight, or blow, as it is termed, the steam will come out of the cylinder-cocks. Should the face or flange of the valve be worn thin, then the pressure may force the valve to be tight when not in motion. The blow, when the flanges are thin, trembles, caused by the vibration of the valve.

If the blow is in the packing, it can be detected by watching the cylinder-cocks. If the blow continues throughout the stroke, when working full-stroke, it will be in the packing. It may also be told by the sound of exhaust, by watching the stroke of piston.

If stuck in a snow bank, and the water becomes low in the boiler, disconnect the front ends of parallel-rods, and oil well the rails and forward driving-wheels. The wheels can now be slipped, to fill the boiler, with both pumps, with little or no damage, either to rail or tire.

It often occurs that the check-valve becomes stuck up, as it is termed, meaning that the valve is off its seat, caused by something getting between the valve-face and valve-seat, or between the side of valve and valve-cage bars, so that there is a free communication between the boiler and pump, giving the pressure of steam in boiler on pump-valve; also heating up the pump to such a degree that the pump-plunger has no action, in regard to receiving or discharging water, the plunger working open the elasticity of the steam in the pump. To get the pump to work, the steam must be condensed in the pump, and the temperature reduced. As soon as the temperature of pump becomes less than 120° Fahrenheit. the pump will commence working.

To cool the pump throw water on the pump and ingress pipe, or by closing the pump feed from tender, and putting the heater on full; then open the pet-cock until the hot water is entirely blown out of pump, close the heater-cock, and put the pump on full. The water coming in contact with the steam that is left in the feed-pipe, after the heater has been shut off, will form a partial vacuum, which will assist the flow of water from the tank to the pump, and cool the pump sufficiently to cause it to start working. Generally, the superfluous matter will be removed from the check-valve shortly after the pump starts to work. The check-valve might be removed altogether from the check-chamber, so far as the benefits derived, while the pump is working. When running at a moderate rate of speed, the pump would work the same. The check-valve gives the same support to the pump that it does to the injector, when not in use. The check-valve prevents the steam and hot water from flowing from the boiler to the pump, when the pump is not working; also giving the same protection to the injector, enabling it to be always ready for duty, when the check-valve is in order.

When taken off or putting on the cylinder-head and steam chest covers, care must be taken to sla k the nuts all around. When tightening them up, the joints should be fair, and the nuts all set down slightly before they are tightened up firmly. If tightened up on one side first there is danger of breaking the cover.

When lining and keying up the main rod it is very important that the same length of rod be retained, in spite of the wear of the brasses, for there is danger of the piston striking against the cylinder-head, as the clearance is very small, sometimes not exceeding $\frac{3}{16}$ inch on each end, which is done to economize fuel and steam. The cross-head should be moved with a bar (before the main rod is attached) until the piston strikes the cylinder-head. To find the amount of clearance allowed for each end of cylinder, scribe a line on the slides for the cross-head to travel, when attached to the main rod.

The driving-box wedges are another important part of the Locomotive Engine, and require to be kept properly adjusted, so that the wheel centres are the same tram or distance apart. The forward wedges of the main drivers should not be altered, only when squaring up the engine, which is seldom needed more than once a year.

The petticoat pipe may be properly adjusted by observing the flame in the furnace. If the petticoat be too high there will be no flame at the furnace door, and the flame will look dark and smoky, and the greater part of the flame and heat will pass through the bottom flues, leaving the top flues to be stopped up with ashes, for the want of draught to keep them open. If the petticoat be too low, then the flame will roll out of the furnace door, when open, and will cause the furnace door to become very hot, when shut; and the greater draught will pass through the top flues, causing the bottom flues to stop up for the want of draught through them. When the petticoat pipe is properly located, the flame will flicker out of the furnace door, when open; and there will be an equal draught through the flues, and they will generally keep open, and the flame will look white like, and full of bright sparks. When the smoke comes out of furnace door, it is evident that the difficulty lies in the top of the stack: the netting being too fine, or the cone too large; otherwise there is not sufficient height from top of straight part of stack to bottom side of cone. All engines have sufficient heating surface. and will generate all the steam required, if the stack and petticoat pipe be properly proportioned and correctly set.

There is one more item to which I will call attention, in regard to keeping an engine on the road some length of time without having to go in the shop for new rod brasses, etc.; that is, to let well enough alone. Never drive a key unless there is need of it; and always drive them when they need to be driven.

FIRST LOCOMOTIVES.

The first Locomotive (or street wagon) on record, is credited to Oliver Evans, of Philadelphia, in the year 1804; the wheels being driven by belts running on pulleys attached to the outer side of the wheels.

George Stevensons' Locomotive "Rocket," was built in the year 1829, at Manchester, England.

The first Locomotive in America, "John Bull," was built in England, in 1830.

The first trip, run by Horatio Allen, (connected with the Novelty Works, of New York City,) who set up the engine, and run it on the Mohawk and Hudson River Road, in the year 1831.

Locomotive "Ironsides" built at Baldwin's works, Philadelphia, Pa., in the year 1832.

——:o:——

IMPORTANT INVENTIONS OF LOCOMOTIVES.

The Locomotive boiler, as now in use, was invented by M. Sequin, an engineer of Annonnay, France, in the year 1828.

The petticoat, or lift-pipe, was invented by Mr. Mathew, about the year 1849.

The use of a separate cut-off valve was patented by Wm. Norris and S. H. Long, December 30, 1833.

T'.e first centre bearing truck has been credited to Wm. S. Hudson, Supt. Rogers Locomotive Works, Paterson, N. J., as early as 1838.

The first four-driving-wheel connected-engine, without a truck, is cred:ted to Henry R. Campbell, of New Hampshire, in 1839.

The equalizing beam was patented by Harrison and Eas wick, of Philadelphia, Pa., in the year 1838 or 1839.

The use of four eccentrics was patented by William Norris and C. H. Long, of Philadeiphia, Pa., in the year 1833.

The bonnet pipe was patented by Leonard Phleger, in the year 1840, then of the Ph:ladelphia and Baltimore Road.

William Norris, o' Philadelphia, Pa., has the credit of applying the first steam whistle to the Locomotive "Carlisle," built for the Cumberland Valley Road, in the year 1834.

Shaıp and Roberts counterbalanced driving-wheels in 1837.

George S. Griggs, of the Boston and Providence Road, used counterbalances in 1838, without knowing of Sharp's application.

The variable independent cut-off was patented by E. Rogers, of Cleveland, Ohio, in 1849.

The first ten-wheel engine built in America, was made by Norris Brothers, Philadelphia, Pa., in 1847.

Walter McQueen has the credit of using the first air chamber on a pump, in 1846.

The self-adjusting, or equalizing truck of a Locomotive, was invented by John L. White, in 1849, now master mechanic on the E. and C. Railroad, at Evansville, Ind.

The link was first used on the Great Western Railway, England, and patented by Mr. Gooch, in 1843.

The link was introduced in the United States by Mr. Howe, (a workman from Robert Stephenson & Co.'s shop, of Newcastle, England), in 1843.

There are more than a score of men claiming to have been the first to use the heater pipes, for protecting the pumps from freezing. We believe heater pipes were used by Uncle Joe Woods, on the Paterson and Hudson River Railroad, when there were but very few railroads in this country.

The American combination, or swing truck was patented by Levi Bissell, in 1858; A. F Smith, in 1862; and Wm. S. Hudson, in 1864.

The blower has been used on the Locomotive, to increase the draught, when not using steam, since 1850; many claiming to have been the first to use it. There have been four patents taken out on the blower since 1857,

FASTEST TIME ON RECORD.

The following fast time has been recorded as having been made on different roads:

Ten miles in 8 minutes; Hamburgh to Buffalo, Lake Shore and Erie Road.

Fourteen miles in 11 minutes, with locomotive and 6 cars; New York Central Road.

Eighteen miles in 15 minutes; Paddington to Slough, England.

Twenty-six miles in 33 minutes; Springfield, Mass., to Hartford, Ct.; N. H. H. and S. Road.

Seventy-one miles in 78 minutes; locomotive and directors' car; Syracuse to Fairport; New York Central Road.

Ninety-one miles in 90 minutes; special train; Janesville to Chicago; Illinois Central Road.

Eighty-one miles in 82 minutes; special train; Rochester to Syracuse; New York Central Road.

Three hundred and five miles in 452 minutes; Albany to Niagara Falls; New York Central Road.

If the above report of time made, be correct, when making 10 miles in 8 minutes, with a 5-foot 6-inch wheel, the valves would have opened and closed, for admission and exhaustion of steam, for both cylinders, 3,060 times per minute. Number of exhausts made per minute, 1,530. Number of times steam admitted to cylinder per minute 1,530. Revolutions made per minute, 382.5. Number of feet piston travels per minute, 1,530.

THE RAILROADS OF THE WORLD.

Interesting facts concerning the railroads of the world. European lines are taken up to a very recent date—31st July, 1874—while those of other lines refer to 1873. From these data it appears that the total lengths of the railways of the world are as follows:

Europe has 81,093 English miles of railroads; America 78,459; Asia 6,049; Africa 1,119, and Australia 1,420. Of the various countries in Europe, Great Britain had, in 1872, in round figures, 16,000 miles of railroad, or 505½ miles to every one million of people. The German Empire came next, with a total length of 15,000 miles, or 370 to each million of people. Then comes France, with 12,000 miles, or 341½ to the million. Then Russia, with 10,500 miles, or 149 to the million people. Then Austria, with 10,200 miles, or 285½ to the million of population. Italy has 4,100 miles; Spain 3,300; Belgium 2,100; Sweden 1,496; Holland and Luxembourg 1,161; Switzerland 936; Turkey 828; Roumania 598; Portugal 522; Norway 308; and Greece only 7. Great Britain has the greatest mileage of railroad, compared with population, and Greece the least. Russia is very low compared with Great Britain, 149 miles to the million, while Great Britain has 505½. Belgium, however, has the greatest mileage, compared with territory, being as 70 to 50 miles to the square "kilo."

MISCELLANEOUS.

Number of Locomotives running in the United States, in the Fall of 1873, 14,000.

Heaviest Locomotive on record, is the "Pennsylvania," on the Reading Railroad, weight 60 tons; diameter of cylinder 20 inches; stroke 26 inches; of the consolidated pattern; being 12 wheels connected; no truck; driving-wheels 4 feet in diameter.

Wide rails.—It has been proved that an engine will pull more cars on the flat-head rail, and the tires wear longer than on a narrow, or round-top rail.

Movement of piston, in relation to the movement of engine.—The first inch of stroke the engine moves six times as far, while the piston is making the first inch ot stroke, as when making the middle inch; the second inch of stroke a little over twice as far; the third inch a trifle over one and one-half times; the fourth inch a trifle less than one and one-half times; the last inch the engine will move a trifle less than it does in making the first inch. This difference is caused by the crank traveling a greater distance, while the piston is moving the first half of stroke, than it does when moving the last half of stroke. If we select the inclined plane, to compare with the action of the crank, (as the principle involved in it is quite similar to the power exerted and transmitted by the crank), we learn that the last inch of the stroke exerts as much force as any other inch of the stroke; but the pressure on the crank at any moment, or at any one point of the last inch of the stroke, is less than at any moment of the middle of stroke. The engine cannot start a load with the same ease when the piston is at the end of stroke, as when it is in the middle of stroke.

Water level on grades.—In ascending an 80-foot grade the water will be 3 inches higher at the fire-box than at the front end, supposing the boiler to be 17 feet long, from front flue sheet.

The safest seat in a railroad train is in the middle of the middle car. There are some chances of danger that are the same anywhere in the train; but others are least in the above-named place.

Does the top of a driving-wheel of a Locomotive travel faster than the bottom, when rolling along the rail?—We would answer that it does. For an illustration: if there be a perpendicular line scribed on the face of the wheel, passing through the centre of axle, from the point where the tire touches the rail, to the highest point of face of tire, and another line scribed on the rail corresponding with the mark on the face of tire; if we now roll the wheel $\frac{1}{16}$th of a revolution on the rail, and drop a line from the mark scribed on the top of wheel to the rail, we find that the bottom of the wheel has only traveled $\frac{1}{36}$th of the distance that the top of the wheel has traveled. And when the wheel has made $\frac{1}{8}$th of a revolution, by dropping a line as before, from the mark made on top of wheel to the rail, we find the top of wheel has traveled 21 times the distance that the bottom has traveled. And at ¼ of a revolution 4½ times as far. Then, again, if we scribe a line across the face of wheel, passing through the centre of axle horizontally with the rail, we find, by moving the wheel $\frac{1}{16}$th of a revolution, that the side of wheel that is ascending has traveled 50 per cent. further than the side that is descending. And at ⅛th of a revolution, the side ascending has traveled 125 per cent. further distance. And at ¼ turn 350 per cent. further distance. At ⅜, 515 per cent. further distance. And, when the wheel has made ½ a revolution, we find, by dropping a line to the rail from the mark made on the tire, that the top of wheel has traveled 451 per cent. greater distance on the rail than the bottom has traveled. The line on face of wheel is now horizontal, for the top to ascend again.

Movement of the wheel.—The wheel does not describe a circle when rolling along on the road, but sweeps an arc of a circle; the radius of the arc is 3½ times the diameter of the wheel. If a pencil or scribe be fixed to the edge of tire, so as to scribe the movement of the wheel, on a board or paper fixed for the purpose, the lines scribed will be like the following diagram:

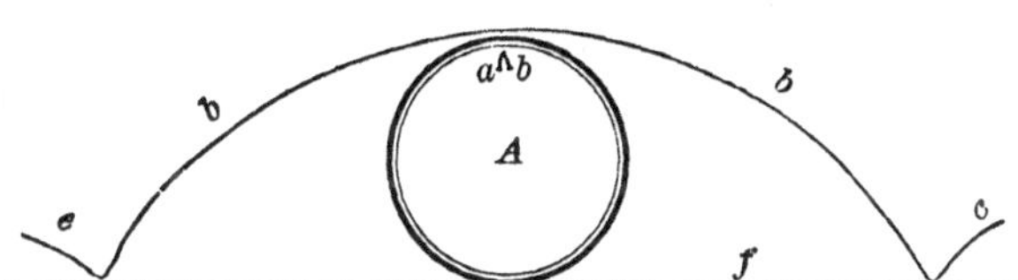

A the wheel; *b b* the arc scribed, with pencil attached to edge of tire; *c* the commencing of the preceding arc; *e* the terminus of arc; *ab*, at the top of wheel, indicates the pencil scribing the arc; *f f* the rail. It will be observed that the wheel scribes the arc from the rail, that being the centre of gravity; the centre being a shifting centre, changing the centre while scribing the arc.

Question.—If each of two Locomotives can pull 80,000 pounds, on a dead pull, and they are connected and draw in opposite directions, what will be the strain on the draw-bar between them? Answer.—80,000 pounds.

Crank at half stroke.—When the piston is at half stroke the crank is not at right angles with the centre line of engine. The crank-pin goes farther during one-half of the stroke of the piston than in the other halt.

Pressure on the crank-pin.—The average pressure on the crank-pin, throughout a revolution, is less than ⅔ of that on the piston with which it is connected; for the crank pin goes more than one-half as far again, at a revolution, than the length of two strokes of the piston.

Weighing an engine under steam.—An engine weighs more on the track, if blowing off steam; the reaction of the steam against the air weights the engine down. In case of an explosion, where the upper part of the boiler gives away, the reaction is so great as to bend down, and even break the rails.

Pressure on the slides.—In running an engine forward the cross-head presses upward all the time; in going backward the pressure is downward.

If the steam is blown from the boiler at the pressure of 15 pounds, or over, the hand may be borne in it without experiencing any inconvenience. When the steam emerges so slow as to have time to condense, its latent heat is given off, and it will scald.

Fulcrum of driving-wheels.—The fulcrum of pressure is at the centre of the wheel, and not on the rail. An engine will start no heavier lead with the crank up, than if it be down, at same angles.

Pressure of the pump valves.—There is no more pressure in the pump than in the boiler, but a glass air vessel, on a Locomotive pump, showed that the air was more compressed when the pump was running slow, and the valves came down to their seats at every stroke, than when the pump was going fast, and the valves did not come quite down. The under side of the valve is about two-thirds as large as the top; yet it must have a total pressure on the bottom more than equal to that on the top, in order to raise it up; the pressure on the valve is equal to the area of opening of water passage.

Heat in Locomotive furnace.—Wood 2,800°; bituminous coal, 3,000°; anthracite coal, 3,300°. The air admitted by the draft to the furnace is expanded to about six times its original volume.

INDEX.

—— :o: ——

A.

Page.

Admission of Steam to Cylinder,..........................80

Area of Cylinder,..........................19

do Circle,..........................16

do Exhaust Port,..........................55

do Flues,..........................24

do Fire Grate,..........................48

do Heating Surface,..........................49

do Triangles,..........................14

do Safety Valves,..........................23

do Steam Port,..........................54

Apothecary Weight,..........................7

Avoirdupois Weight..........................7

B.

Boiler Construction,..........................68

Brass Composition,..........................37

Boiler Leaking,..........................159

Boiler, length of,..........................48

Beer Measure,..........................10

Boiler Staying,..........................69

Boiler Pressure,..........................32

Branch Pipe,..........................54

Boiler, washing out,..........................159

Boiler, gallons of water in,..........................59, 63, 67, 77

C.

Page.
Compression, ...98
Clearance,........................81
Circumference of Circle,........................15
Choking an Engine,........................159
Cubical Contents of Water in Boiler,........................51
Counter-balancing Driving Wheels,........................39
Case Hardening,........................38
Construction of Locomotive,........................99
Crank Movement,........................179
Circular Measure,........................13
Counter Pressure,........................98
Crank Pin,........................56
Check Valve,........................166

D.

Diameter of Branch Pipe,........................54
Diameter of Circles, ...16
Degrees of Heat in Furnace........................181
Duty of an Engineer,........................155
Diameter of Steam Dome,........................48
Decimal of an Inch,........................22
Decimal of a Foot,........................23
Dry Measure,........................11
Dimensions of parts of Locomotive,........................47
Diameter of Steam Pipe,........................54
Diameter of Piston Rod,........................55
Duty when off the track,........................59

E.

Eccentric,........................78
Exhaust Clearance,........................68
Eccentric, position of,........................86, 110, 160
Engine, having a pound,........................165

F.

Page.

Framing,..72
Friction of Cars,..46
Firing Engine,...155
First Locomotive,...171
Fast Time,..174

G.

Grades, table of,..26

H.

Heating Surface,..49, 63, 67
Heating Surface of Flues,..63, 67
Heaviest Locomotive,..176
Horse Power, per hour,...47
How to Weigh Safety Valve,...50

I.

Important dimensions of Locomotive,...............................61
do Inventions of parts of Locomotive,..........................171

L.

Lap,...92
Lead,...93
Lead, Premature,..99
Lead, increase of,..94
Lead on Exhaust,..99
Lateral Motion,...82
Link Motion,...83
Long Measure,...8
Length of Main Rod,...101
do Parallel Rod,...102
do Rocker Arm,...102

Page.
Length of Valve Rod,..........103
do Eccentric Rod,..........104
do Reach Rod,.......... 105
Lining up Rods,..........162

M.

Moulding and Casting,..........78
Miscellaneous Measures,..........112
Metal between Ports,..........55
Measure of Time,..........12
Mensuration of Solids,..........17
Mensuration of Surface,..........13
Movement of Valve with Piston,..........153

N.

Number of Locomotives,..........176

P.

Packing,..........162
Piston,..........56
Pumping Engine,..........157
Prevent Foaming,..........163
Power of Locomotive,..........42
Premature Lead,..........99
Petticoat Adjustment,..........168
Piston Rod,..........55
Piston having blow or leak,..........165
Pressure on Slides,..........180
Point of Suspension,..........89

R.

Radius of Link,..........88
Radius of Curves,..........32

Page.
Resistance of Grades,..26
Resistance of Trains,.......................................25, 30
Railroads of the World,......................................175
Revolutions of Driving Wheels, per hour,........................29

S.

Speed of Pistons,..21
Safety Valve Lever,..50
Setting an Eccentric,...110
Steam Dome,.. 71
Slip of Link,..88
Stopping Leaks of Boiler,.....................................159
Square Measure,...9
Steam Pipe Bursting,..162
Safety Plug,...57
Shrinkage of Steel Tire,.......................................39
Steam used at one revolution,.................................129
Safety Valve,..49
Safety Valve Lever,..50
Setting up Wedges,..168

T.

Tender,..75
Thickness of Bridges,..55
Throttle Detached,..163
Throw of Eccentric,..53
Table of Flue Surface,...24
do Steam Temperature,..27
do Speeds,...29
do Laps and Lead,...154
do Movement of Valve,...153
Time Table,..35
Tractive Power,..45
Travel of Valve,...53

Page.

Throttle Valve,..80

Troy Weight,...7

Table of Link Motion,...115

do No. 1, without Lap, Lead $\frac{1}{8}$ inch,..................................115

do No. 2, Lap $\frac{3}{8}$ inch, Lead 1-16 inch,.......................................117

do No. 3, Lap $\frac{3}{8}$ inch, Lead $\frac{3}{8}$ inch,...................................119

do No. 4, Lap $\frac{5}{8}$ inch, Lead, 5-16 inch,....................................121

do No. 5, Lap $\frac{7}{8}$ inch, inside Lap $\frac{1}{8}$ inch, Lead 3-16 forward motion, back motion blind, having $\frac{1}{8}$ inch less than no lead,...123

Table No. 6, Lap $\frac{7}{8}$ inch, inside Lap $\frac{1}{8}$, Lead 1-16 inch....... 125

do No. 7, Lap 1 inch, inside Lap $\frac{1}{4}$, Lead 1-16 inch,........127

do No. 8, Lap 1 inch, inside line-and-line, Lead 1-16 inch, 129

do No. 9, Lap $\frac{3}{4}$ inch, inside line-and-line, throw of eccentric $4\frac{1}{2}$ inch, Lead 1-16 inch, ...131

do No. 10, Lap $\frac{3}{4}$ inch, inside line-and-line, throw of eccentric $6\frac{1}{4}$ inches, Lead 1-16 inch,..................................133

do No. 11, Lap $\frac{5}{8}$ inch inside line-and-line, Lead $\frac{1}{8}$ inch,..135

do No. 12, same as No. 11,..137

do No. 13, same at No's. 11 and 12,.................................138

do No. 14, Lap $\frac{3}{4}$ inch, inside lap 1-16 inch, Lead $\frac{1}{8}$ inch, 140

do No. 15, same as No. 14,..141

do No. 16, same as No.'s 14 and 15,.................................143

do No. 17, Lap $\frac{3}{4}$ inch, inside Lap $\frac{1}{8}$ inch, Lead 1-16 inch, 144

do No. 18, Lap $\frac{3}{4}$ inch, inside line-and-line Lead 1-16 inch, 146

do No. 19, Lap $\frac{3}{4}$ inch, inside 1-16 inch, Lead 1-16 inch,.147

do No. 20, Lap $\frac{3}{4}$ inch, inside $\frac{1}{4}$ inch, Lead 1-16 inch,......149

do No. 21, Lap $\frac{3}{4}$ inch, inside 1-16 inch, Lead $\frac{1}{8}$ inch,......150

Tables No.'s 5 & 6 showing effect of taking lead of back motion, and increasing lead on forward motion.

Tables No.'s 7 & 8, showing effect of inside lap.

Tables No.'s 9 & 10, showing the effect of increasing the throw of eccentric.

Tables No.'s 11 & 12, showing the effects of changing point of suspension.

Tables No.'s 11 & 13, changing length of stroke; 14 & 15, changing working centres.
Tables No.'s 15 & 16, changing position of lifting shaft.
Tables No.'s 8 & 18, show the effect of lap.

V.

Page.
Valve without lap, ... 91
do with lap on lap line, ... 97
do on lead line, ... 109
do showing full opening of port, ... 113
do Blow, ... 165
do setting, ... 104

W.

Weight of Locomotive, ... 59, 77
Working with one cylinder, ... 164
Wine Measure, ... 10
Wheel Movement, ... 179
Weight on Driving Wheels, ... 73
Wheels and Tire, ... 74
Water in Boiler, ... 59 & 77
Weight of Rails per mile, ... 22
Wrist Pin of Cross-head, ... 56
Weight of Tender, ... 59 & 75

www.ingramcontent.com/pod-product-compliance
Lightning Source LLC
LaVergne TN
LVHW011223110826
845150LV00006B/1521

9781425516000